RRAJ's GUIDE
for
FRESHMEN

ROBERT REXFORD ANIM JNR (RRAJ)

RRAJ's GUIDE FOR FRESHMEN.

Edited by Mr Eric Okyere and Mr Kwadwo Amo Osei

Typeset by Apenteng Kwaku Kusi

Cover Design by Emmanuel Osei Agyemang

Self-published in Ghana 2021.

Printed by Graduate Standard Printing and Secretarial Services

ISBN: 978-9988-3-1055-4

For enquiries mail to: robertrexford@icloud.com or

Contact +233 (0) 248 097313

For Purchases Contact +233 (0) 245 077425

DEDICATION

I dedicate this book to my lovely wife, Mrs Irene Anim.

To my Parents, Robert Rexford Anim and Juliana Boadu and my siblings; Evelyn Aboagye, Anim Kojo Fosu and Aning Poakwah.

ACKNOWLEDGEMENT

Albeit, this book bears the name of an individual, it is the work of a dedicated team. There is this book because of the contribution, assistance and sacrifices of many individuals.

First of all, I thank my perfect half, Mrs Irene Anim for the love, support and assistance on this journey.

I extend my gratitude to Mr Eric Okyere, my editor who took the time to take me on the writing journey and helped me accomplish this milestone.

I am also indebted to Mr Amo Osei (Ex Registrar, Presbyterian University College, Abetifi) for taking his time to revise the final draft before publication.

I am grateful to Mr Daniel Amenuvor Yaw Mawuli Edulah, Mrs Priscilla Essah, Mr Richard Ahazi, and Hanes Kudjo Sterling for sharing their experiences to inspire the next generation.

I thank all my peer reviewers; Mrs. Matilda Akosua Boahemaa, Mabel Omane Darkwah, Edward Aning Poakwah, Mr Adansi Kofi and Mrs Emmanuella Adansi, Lewisa Oppong, Mr Mark Addai Kwarteng, Elvis Dela Gbena, Ishmael Bekoe, Thomas Asare, Prince Amewugah, John Dogbe Simplicity, Nehemiah Afful and Patience Amo Osei for dedicating their valuable time to read the draft.

To everyone who contributed in any way, thank you. May the almighty God bless you all for your immense support.

TABLE OF CONTENTS

PREFACE

When I realized that I had free time on my hand during my national service at the Town and Country Planning Department, TCPD, Ho Municipal Assembly, I created a google form which asked five things graduates wished they had known before entering the University and also, five things that they wish they had learnt before completing tertiary. The honest responses that I received began the journey of **RRAJ's Guide for Freshmen**. I started writing and also, while sending out transcripts to colleagues, friends and family for review. I had assistance from Eric Okyere, after we met at a Springboard Road Show program and he became a key instrument to the completion of the manuscript. Mr Amo Osei took his time to review every sentence to enhance its readability and clearly convey the message it carried. The manuscript continually went through reviews from academia, religious groups, students and online book clubs to ensure it meets the needs of the 21st century tertiary students.

I believe a book will elude fear, in any form, that may limit access to the information, knowledge or assistance people may need.

This book is a letter to my old self as a freshman on the campus of the Kwame Nkrumah University of Science and Technology (KNUST) in Ghana narrating how I could have approached it differently, taken advantage of opportunities and graduated with much fulfillment. I am passionate about it because it will become an instrumental aid for tertiary students and answer the numerous questions that cross the minds of the many young people who come into the University naïve and ignorant, like I was about a decade ago.

I am proud today not because I have written a book but for the reason that, in the years to come, there will be graduates who have been imparted by the system, taken advantage of most opportunities and are confident in themselves as change agents.

INTRODUCTION

It was one Friday that I had to move into a new environment that was temporal and for a call that ought to be answered. A time I had waited for years has come but I could not savour a moment. I went into the high-rise environment where ambitions are accustomed to being fulfilled.

I had gotten admission into the Kwame Nkrumah University of Science and Technology (KNUST) to pursue BSc. Human Settlement Planning. I was very happy and auspicious about this journey. Before I bought my admission forms, I talked to a cousin who had completed KNUST and a long distant family member who graduated from the University of Ghana (UG). They coached me on how to fill the forms and decided on the choice of programmes. They were helpful throughout the processes and equally there for me after admission. What they couldn't do for me was, to enlighten me on the journey that I was about to embark, take the challenge on my behalf, teach me how develop and implement a plan. I was left to immerse myself in the adventure and I must co nfess, it was unpleasant.

I wished I understood that being free was where I had to be the most responsible in my life. There are decisions I took and wish I had taken alternatives instead. There were opportunities I could have taken advantage only if I knew they existed. There were networks I should have created, only if I found them important then. I was not exposed to some important information which was vital for my academic success. For example, I had no idea about the grading system and how it worked. I wasn't interested in my programme but took it out of pity, I didn't understand credit hours. My first year at the university was in total shambles and confusion. All that I understood was wake up, check the timetable and go for lectures, study small, make friends, have fun and let's make a degree.

A wider Experience

Priscilla was denied a BSc. Business Administration but given settlement planning so she pursued it out of pity. Stress and lack of interest nearly made her quit. She later found her purpose, redefined her mindset and took upon a challenge to be the best student she has always been. Although Priscilla started as a second-class upper student, she ended up graduating as the best student in her college. She went on to do her Master's degree at Cambridge University.

Richard was also a Geography student of the University of Cape Coast. After gaining admission, Richard realized that his school's academic calendar was quite different and demanding. He did not give up on his academic goals but adjusted his old style to suit the challenging academic style of the institution.

Hanes Sterling also gives us a gist of how he used his free time as a student on campus. Hanes studied Computing and business information technology at the University of Greenwich (UK collaboration with Intercom Programming Manufacturing Company (IPMC) Institute of Technology), although his course was demanding and challenging, he used his free time and long vacations to expand his knowledge through self-education. These and other inspiring stories are what have filled this book.

Purpose Await

I read "Purpose Driven Life[1]" by Rick Warren while writing this book and at the moment I needed an introduction. I was late catching up a bus from Accra to Ho but only to be told it was full. I had to take an alternative one which was expensive. I saw the book on the middle seat of the car I boarded afterwards, checked the title and kept it on my lap until the owner surfaced. It was the driver's and I opted to take a glance. I took Rick's forty day's journey on purpose discovery afterwards and wished to have met it earlier. I realised we are part of a bigger picture and what God intends for each of us is just a bit. I was touched by each sentence in the book and most importantly a perfect idea for an introduction for this book. A disappointment of not getting an affordable bus with the anger of paying more led to the puzzle I had been trying to solve for over two months.

I have realised that it is never too late to start that bigger dream. Your dedication and pursuance are key to every success but not time. Time is a little switch aid to what is next on the to-do list of men. Focus on each listing on your plan which is vital to the success of each goal. You have chosen a path; your determination and submission will lead the way. Each human being has different goals in life but we are all in this world. With different programmes and career plans, the school you find yourself plays a central role in the journey. Considering the age of the current university students, this level climaxes one adolescent age and paves way for adulthood. They struggle to climax the youthful exuberance as well as being well informed, enlightened and matured for the future

---

[1] Warren, R. (2002). *Purpose-Driven Life: What on Earth Am I here for?* Zondervan, Grand Rapids, Michigan

that awaits. Finding a balance then becomes a problem because the more you give in to the former the lesser, you're informed for the latter and vice versa. You can achieve that balance by self-definition. Knowing yourself will help you to redefine your priorities and focus on the important tasks ahead. Before what is provided in this Guide, I need to tell you something to keep you mindful and pave the way to the new beginning.

In this episode of life that you await to be transformed to undertake responsibilities, get time for your true self. Weigh every influence and assess all your capabilities, identify where you fall short and start replenishing. Do not weaken the foundation you will build your future on at this stage but erect a Jericho wall that one only God can dismantle. Dr Myles Munroe's word to us, the third worlds is a turnaround in our attitudes[2]. You can change the world no matter your colour, location or environment. The only need is a renewed mindset. It is not about how you want people to see or think about you but how truly you are; that will make a great impact. What you see is a reflection of the true self when you are in front of a mirror but not after the makeup. Your thoughts will mature to be you tomorrow but not what a friend thinks. You can recoup what you have lost by a changed mindset and what you choose to accept or neglect will be your new reality. At the tertiary level, you have the freedom, time and resources at your pace as a student which you will not get in the house or elsewhere as a freebie. Harness every opportunity that can help you in school.

This world has been developed not only from its best decision or moments but from its toughest challenges. Savour every beautiful moment and embrace every problem as it will

---

[2] Munroe, M. (2011). *Spirit of leadership*. Whitaker house, New Kensington

strengthen you for the challenges ahead. You can always get solutions to your problems, but it will only empower you to be dependent, but creating solutions make you a man/woman of great value. Do not hesitate to ask the toughest questions about everything you need to know because it is a necessity to be well informed for the future.

In the next chapters, you will obtain the keys and guides that hold every secret to help you discover your purpose as a student and the lessons to prepare you for the future that awaits.

Who Is This Book For?

There has never been a perfect moment for success. Achievers take advantage of their environments and turn challenges into opportunities. The goal of this book, like Simon Sinek's "Start with why[3]" is not to fix the current challenges of the tertiary institutions. Rather, I'm sharing experiences to help you understand the tertiary level and know that what you will face is not different so rise up to the occasion. This guide will help you focus on the things that worked for others to achieve success amidst the challenges.

How this Book is structured

The book is into four parts, the first section is the keys for your purpose definition. It will help you understand your new environment and assist you to make the necessary provision that will be needed for the journey. This level is different from where you have been, therefore, the need for such enlightenment. Planning, why you need you to challenge

---

[3] Sinek, S. (2011). Start with why. Penguin Books

yourself, examination structure and research are all discussed in this section.

The second part elaborates on resources on your campus to help in your academic, personal and careers lives. The third section of this book contains the lessons to set you on the path to becoming a graduate worth the tag. The lessons will help you maximize your time as a student by learning something new, creating valuable networks, building a career or a business, managing your finances effectively, empower a female colleague and other valuable lessons important on this journey.

The last section presents the guides which includes assignment/coursework guide, presentation guide, and teamwork, working with your academic tutors and relationship and lifestyle on campus.

I have tried my best to include every valuable information throughout my three years of research to make this level in your educational cycle a simple and enjoyable journey. You may not need another guide but if you want to go further, a list of notes is added to the appendices. As this guide seeks to give you an insight on your tertiary journey, there is less on theories and others input not to complicate things but I have included valuable references on each page to assist you discover more. A special website will also be dedicated to all the resources you need throughout your tertiary journey.

PART ONE:

KEYS

CHAPTER ONE

FIND YOUR PURPOSE

- ❖ Purpose, find one
- ❖ The five critical areas

This chapter will guide you on what to consider essential on your journey to help you build a stronger foundation for your purpose definition.

Purpose, Find one

It is difficult to attain a milestone in life without purpose. John C. Maxwell[4] assert that you need to believe, develop passion, and make initiatives, be focused, prepare and practice, to achieve results. A man without a sense of purpose in life lacks the character and potential to be successful in what s/he pursues.

You need a reason to wake up every dawn and revise your lecture notes, undertake a research or learn a skill while you roommates are sleeping. You need a reason to skip a move night or remain single while your friends are mingling. When you find a purpose, it become the passion that drives you and the energy that precedes your actions. You purpose become a burning desire that ought to be quenched.

Your financial or social standing will not define your purpose as a student but what you recreate and put your mind to achieve become your new reality

---

[4] Maxwell, J. C. (2011). *Beyond talent: become someone who gets extraordinary results.* Thomas Nelson, Nashville.

A key need to help you at this level is to be clear with why you're schooling. To find your purpose as a student, you need to understand the conditions you will meet as a student to be able to face the challenges ahead with enthusiasm.

THE CRITICAL AREAS TO HELP YOU FIND YOUR PURPOSE AS A STUDENT

The Tussle between your Freedom and Responsibility

Dr Myles Munroe wrote that "Freedom and Power" are the two most important elements in life. Power needs responsibility while freedom needs laws. Your school gives you the ultimate freedom and many laws. Thus, by being responsible, you are obtaining the power to define, plan, initiate, focus, practice, preserve, till you attain. The means of attaining your tertiary goals will be discussed in the next two chapters. Before that, you need to define why you are a student and take responsibility to achieve it. This should be your first critical area to consider. This gives you the power to achieve. The tertiary level is the stage in the educational cycle that you will be given the utmost freedom to manage your affairs. Your actions are your initiates. Who you keep as friends, how your money is spent and time to study is your own decision.

The test of your maturity is how you handle your freedom. How do you manage your time effectively to suit your books and other activities fighting for your attention? How do you handle friends and still be your true self?
Do you want to pass or fail your first responsibility exam?

The tertiary level comes with unending experience and presents the toughest challenges. For this reason, you need to cultivate the habit of taking responsibility. Will your freedom be managed to improve ruin your future? Note that every decision that you take will affect your future. It is, therefore, imperative for you to use this freedom for yourself. The important thing is for you to understand the role you need to play to ensure your success as a student. Developing effective Lecturer–Student's relations, sound decision making, time and resource management are key responsibilities in that quest.

Your programme will be very demanding

I can testify that at this level, no single course is a haven for the lazy person. You have to sacrifice, adapt and learn to know what has become part of you. Every student has attended a senior high school or its equivalent level, written several exercises and examinations before reaching the tertiary level. You have sailed through all these with determination, dedication and sacrifice and now that you're at this level, there is another bridge to cross.

You may have to break your back at times, neglect some of the old friends, alter your old routine, change sleep pattern learn a new skill or software to succeed with you knew program. Although, may be demanding, it is worth it.

Your hard work paid some time ago, and it will pave the way for you to become the great person you have always envisioned someday. Pray to God, seek his counsel and take inspiration from the strength he gave you in the best moments in your life and this will be nothing more than it.

Every Sitting at this level is a Final Examination

In the primary and high schools, students prepare for final examination through a series of organized assignments, tests and end of term examination.

At the tertiary level, there is nothing like a final examination and every sitting, is the final exam. These few highlighted words are almost all you need to be on top of your academic goals. The assignments, research works, mid-semester examinations, term papers, field reports etc. are cumulatively part of the degree you will be awarded after graduation. You need to approach each one as if you're writing a final examination. You have to face everyone with the passion, charisma, zeal and mentality you used in writing your WASSCE. I didn't know that the first assignment I wrote at the university will determine the final certificate that was handed to me after graduation. Had I known this; I would have tackled every assignment or coursework with my last breath. A low/high mark in one influence the other. A low score in a quiz just because you had to fix relationship issues affects your overall average. The certificate you will be rewarded at the end of your years of study is a cumulative of all the marks obtained in each graded coursework. Your responsibility is to always prepare because the quiz you will write is as important as the end of semester examination.

Effective Time Management
This is a completely different level from other levels in the educational cycle. Your freedom will be full of responsibilities. To meet them, you need to be time conscious. The twenty-four hours in a day will never double for you, so, whatever is on the timetable now, execute it and move on to the next item in line. To be an effective time manager, you need to know

yourself. What are your daily activities, how many lectures will you have within a week, and what should be your study schedule? These will make your list. Put them down and apportion your time to meet them. Set deadlines to help you accomplish tasks. If you leave things anyhow, they will never be accomplished. Time limits will push you to realise what is due at every moment. For example, if you plan to learn graphic designing a semester further, break it down into weekly achievable tasks to enable you to attain that end. Big tasks, projects or goals often scare us. To make them attainable, try and break each into smaller doable tasks based on your interests. Set time limits for each smaller one. Punish yourself if you fail, if that is what it takes to get things done. Set deadlines to accomplish each and watch your dreams come together like magic. To learn how to accomplish more with time, learn how to focus on one thing at a time, get it done and move onto the next on the list.

Understand your grading system

Tertiary institutions in the country have adopted two forms of grading systems thus, Gradient Point Average (GPA) and Cumulative Weighted Average (CWA). University of Ghana (UG) uses the GPA system while Kwame Nkrumah University of Science and Technology (KNUST) uses CWA. Most Technical Universities also use the GPA system. Tertiary institutions use 'weight' in the form of credit hours to determine the importance of a course to your programme. A course, which is assigned a higher credit hour entails more workload, and your score affects your total output for the semester. Credit hours are measured in time. One credit hour course means one hour of lecture time in class per week. This is excluding other laboratory works, field/practical, assignments and projects work as well. A higher mark on courses that wields few credit hours will not improve on your total average, however, a higher mark on a four-credit hour course can increase your average. This is not to give you the indication that don't put in the effort for low credit hours courses but make sure that you always maintain a balance.

Don't be Selfish

I once sat in a car and one of the passengers was advising his younger brother who has gotten admission to the university. One thing that caught my attention was that, tertiary students in general should not be selfish or individualistic with academics or knowledge acquisition. Teamwork play a key role in excelling in all areas. If you keep your presentation skills to yourself while your group members cannot deliver, you will fall as a team. If you are aiming to make the highest mark, a CWA 69.99 and 60.01 or GPA 3.01 and a 3.49 will earn the same class. This is not to say, don't give in your best but just to remind you that, a little assistance to someone who find it difficult with a course will not take your glory nor will the highest mark you obtain be quoted on your certificate.

Although you may be brilliant but without networks and information sources you will always make unnecessary sacrifices. However, creating networks and access to needed information will save you time and even give you opportunities to expand your abilities. You will learn from your team and contribute to general development as a team. You would only deny yourself personal growth opportunities by being selfish.

Key 1

1. What has this chapter taught me?

____

____

____

____

____

2. What other things do I have to be watchful?

____

____

____

____

____

3. What are my responsibilities as a tertiary student?

____

____

____

____

____

____

____

____

CHAPTER TWO

CHALLENGE YOUR PURPOSE

- ❖ *The biggest challenge on campus*
- ❖ *Taking the challenge*

Having defined your purpose, you need to develop what it takes to attain it. In this chapter, you will learn about a persistent challenge most students face and "why" you ought to give what it takes to attain your tertiary goals.

The main challenge to most students is lack of interest in their programme. This sometimes eludes passion thereby resulting in poor academic performance. Everyone on this campus may be facing a challenge. Can you guess the future we are heading if everyone has not been interested in their programmes but just go through the tertiary school system like that? We will be only preparing for a loom. There would be thousands of graduates who can't give practical solutions to emerging challenges. Our leadership may be worse than what we're witnessing. If things are not good now, it won't be better when products of this system take the leadership mantle.

The demanding nature of most programmes also accounts for the lack of the passion. You may not like your programme and its accompanying challenges such as morning lectures, presentations, reports writing, research and field works, etc. I must confess, it is exhausting and demanding. Your life becomes contained around a routine which you're not interested in. Such demanding conditions affect students. If you may not know, it will be new but this revelation should just tell you that that is the status quo. Almost everyone feels he/she has been given the wrong choice. You will sit in class with students who would withdraw after the first year and chase the programmes of their dreams. Many will just go through the system without any positive impact. Few will realise the need, redefine their cause and amass the energy that would have been committed to their programme of choice and come out successful. These few ones will be unstoppable. Will you be one of the few?

John narrated how his mentality and lack of interest in his course affected his academic performance.

I came to school without any knowledge about my programme. I also came after matriculation and mid-semester examinations were around the corner. It was not easy as I initially disliked my programme, but here I am faced with no other option than to pursue a degree in it. Initially, I tried just to manage and complete the degree anyhow but that was not me. I want to win and win well so I sat down and thought about how well to develop a passion for the programme.

I dug deeper into the programme and was enlightened with opportunities that come with it. It virtually changed my perspective of the programme. I resulted in adopting formulae that could enable me to obtain the class of my choice, and I can say, it worked. It's simple, I just go through the day's studies and on weekends take a course and study it starting from the beginning of the semester to where you have reached now. Do it for other courses in that regard and remember it is cyclical.

Always remember where there is no passion, persistence rarely exists. John Dogbe Simplicity, KNUST

Understanding this and putting in your best is important to your success as a student. Collins C. Maxwell discovered that when it comes to academics, there is a greater correlation between self-confidence and academic achievements than what has been established between I.Q. and the latter. Even if you are a brilliant student, your input will have a greater influence on your academic achievement. Your brilliance is just like talent. To Collins C. Maxwell, you need to go beyond it. This is done by developing accompanying traits to expand it. As a student, you ought to understand the role you need to play in your success.

When you graduate, you will be able to work in other fields provided you can add value now.

READY TO TAKE THE CHALLENGE?

Elude the Mindset that the Tertiary Level is Easy

One enemy of perseverance is complacency. The feeling that things will be easy and will always go our way to kill dreams. In the road less travelled, Scott Peck started his book by admitting life to be a difficulty. It is the only truth that can help you face life's most difficult moments.

When you accept that something is difficult, it no longer becomes difficult. Campus life is difficult because you need to do so many things by yourself while developing certain traits and expertise to successfully go through the system. The problems you will face as a tertiary student may be directly related to your studies or personal life, relationships, finance, course materials and even a deadline. Problems will always prevail, but you should know that no matter how bad it may be, there is always a solution. Because you have not discovered one does not mean there is no solution. The more you probe, the better your results. Knowing this will make it easier. When a problem stares in the face, take it easy and be calm, the storm will surely pass.

In becoming Michelle Obama talked about incredible people whom she has met over the years throughout her journey from the Sidley and Austin Law Firm to the White house. They lived happy and flawless lives as if they've gotten every good thing in this world. Some of them were from poor families or raised in conditions that may make many of us but have equally accomplished extraordinary things. The reality is that they had faced the problem, challenges and oppressions as well however, they identified their purposes of existence and became numb to their oppressors. They learn to move forward and draw energy from those who believe in them.

We are all in our battles but manage to smile, celebrate and make merry with others. When you meet a problem, know that beginning this journey is a problem. Do not panic but just relax, accept it and challenge your way to the top. The goals not to quit but to make a degree, a proud one indeed.

What you need now

I understand you may have your reasons for a preferred programme. Probably career goals or your family's line of profession you need to emulate etc. Your reason is highly respected and important but this very moment there is something you need to focus badly. This is your new conferred programme. Love it, pursue it with passion and you will be satisfied with the outcome.

A story by Eric Thomas on one of his motivational broadcasts which were reiterated by Collins C. Maxwell that it is related to Socrates. The story is about one man who went to Socrates and asked him for knowledge. Socrates then led him down the sea to waist-deep water, then pushed him under for about 30 seconds and asked again what he wanted, he replied, knowledge. He did a second time and he reiterated knowledge. He did a third time but this time he prolonged the time he was left underneath the water. The man then forced himself out screaming, "I need air". He realized that although he wanted knowledge, he needed air badly at that particular time. You may want a certain programme of study but here you are with an alternative. What you need now is concentration on what you have been offered and accepted to pursue it. That is all you need for not.

Start with Your Why.

Simon Sinek found a cure to the dying love for his work that paid him so well[5]. There was nothing wrong with him per se. There was not a change in working conditions that may have unfavoured him. Neither his work has been relocated nor gotten a better offer from a competitor. The problem was that he wasn't motivated to wake up each morning to do his

------

[5] Sinek, S. (2011). *Start with why: how great leaders inspire everyone to take action.* Portfolio, USA.

routine; bath, shower, drive to work, stay there and work and return to the house. He realized he has lost the zeal to do it. A sudden turn came and he was able to pick up the pieces together and willing to go back to his work. He found "why". Simon realized that he was initially satisfying what he wanted out of the job, so when he had much, the passion to keep the job faded.

To challenge your purpose, you need to differentiate between **WHAT** brought you from your house to this campus, **HOW** you will go about what you came here for and **WHY** you came. This is the passion that should drive every nerve to satisfy why you are a programme A or B student. The WHY can be the people who inspire you and challenge you to achieve beyond your potential. This is what should drive you but not the money you will gain from your invention, or a job opportunity after obtaining your master's degree etc.

These will define your WHY as a student. It will give you a reason to wake every dawn, exercise, meditate, read and prepare for lectures with high spirits. It will set you in the right direction and undertake critical actions you need to consider if you want to be successful. You may be familiar with some of these keys but without a WHY you would just see them as things that students need to consider but not you specifically. You would see it as the reason to practise what you'll learn in this book. Without why, you will receive the best coaching, take the initiative but when you're just three feet from gold, you will quit because you can't sustain that energy.

Starting with why defines a clear goal, take the necessary action and ensure that it is obtained.

Your new Programme is an Opportunity

The sciences, humanities and arts are all important and contributing immensely to changing the world. The doctor might save lives, but the Agriculturist will help feed him to keep him alive and active. The Artist has made the streets and homes beautiful with their creativity. The architect conceives and the engineer makes it sound with his calculations, and all these grand edifices along our major streets came into being. Before these, the planner has to decide where every single one should be located in space and it is as well with all other significant fields of study. You will become a doctor with your profession, and your work will save lives as well. You will change the world with your intervention in the status quo. You will equally alter the world with the new you, provided you will acquire and be awash with what it takes to do that.

You will be a great addition to the number who have taken this wonderful profession to the world to help make it a better place. We need you there to improve the world when you finally graduate. It is not only a particular programme that will help you realise your dreams, although the programme offered you might deny you a profession but not a life. It is not about the programme but your capabilities or how you use your acquired knowledge to climb the social ladder or make a change is important. The employers recruit competent staff so do not think you will be advantaged with just a certificate. Learn how to become the best in the programme you are pursuing.

Your new Programme is worth your effort
Team of intellects designed every course at this level. They thought about its contribution to humanity, and most

importantly the people who will supervise its implementation in the real world. You are part of the few selected to pursue that new programme implemented by the university or polytechnic. Your mentor might happen to be part of the panel that drew the module, and I know they know better. It went through the scrutiny by a board and finally a decision was made for its implementation. Programmes offered at the tertiary level are cut across all walks of life and an institution will consider its specialty role and resources at disposal to run a particular one. Improving life is at the centre of consideration therefore, courses are modelled toward the betterment of humanity. When students are offered their preferred choice of programme, it motivates them to give their best. Interest gradually fades if it turns out otherwise.

Accepting, understanding and being dedicated will be integral if you would excel with your new course. It is critical to ignite interest by reading more about it. Find out the list of Alumni, scholars and personalities with the programme attached to their success stories, and you will be thrilled. Did you accept the offer out of the blue because you needed to be in school? If no, then the decision comes with a responsibility and not just to attain self-esteem. A field of less interest does not mean it is not important to mankind or a shame to be studied at the tertiary level. If you are anxious to talk to someone who knows more about it. The counselling unit is available, lecturers and continuing students are there to open up to you.

Have you thought of your role model?
I was taken aback the first time I sat in class being tutored by Professor Kwasi Kwafo Adarkwa (ex-Vice-Chancellor of

KNUST) in my first year at the University. As a mentor to many, he inspired and ignited our interest in the programme. He was a figure most freshmen have heard or read about and his presence in the class would exhilarate an organised atmosphere for learning. How he would intrigue the passion for tackling the most challenging task was a spirit each of his students inherited. We are most at times interested in the pleasant successes' stories of our role models but not the tragic journeys they have made prior to such triumphs. You are not the only one in this dilemma because most students hated their programme at a point in time. The longer you keep worrying, the greater your distraction and the less your input. It's mysterious almost everyone looks lost in our institutions at the tertiary level. You sometimes have to take inspiration and console yourself from the cyclical mystery.

The first professional contract I had after school was awarded by someone who studied Geomatics Engineering.
He earlier wanted to pursue planning but had a different programme he perceived to be unfortunate at that time. He accepted the challenge, considered the programme even though the interest was not there and came out successful".
He inspired me with his earlier interest in the course and encouraged us to be proud and put our best in it knowing the opportunities ahead.

It is time to reconsider the decision, accept your unwanted programme and find a reason to challenge your decision.

If you Persist, you can Achieve

Perseverant is all about the result. It is what you have set your mind to attain. It guarantees accomplishment. A persevering person is determined even if all odds are against him/her. He/she completes many short races to reach a destination and only stops when the task is done. To them, every challenge is an opportunity to learn. Most programmes offer opportunities at the second-degree' level to embark further from other related courses except some sciences and health-related ones which you would have to start from the first degree. After the first degree, there is another chance of achieving your dream at the masters' level. You can study a different programme as you could pursue Business Administration although you studied Science at the high school level. **Note** that only candidates who graduate with good degrees can pursue further at the masters (postgraduate) level. Most scholarship programs prefer students with certain class honours. **First-class** and **second-class upper** divisions are better posed for such opportunities.

Also, most research degrees (MPhil) may not accept the second-class lower degree. A **Pass** will not take you anywhere.

Key *2*

1.   What has this chapter taught me?

____

____

____

____

2.   How do I challenge my Purpose?

____

____

____

____

____

____

____

____

____

____

CHAPTER THREE

PLAN YOUR PURPOSE

- ❖ Do you have a Plan?
- ❖ Developing an effective Plan

This chapter will take you through the processes to assist you to bring all the ideas together to create an effective plan.

If you have a list of goals to be achieved, one important thing to consider is your roadmap to get there. A plan states emphatically how to go about a task at hand with the intentions of achieving a result. It is good to have a plan especially as you embark on your tertiary education. You might have thought of it, and by that, you are on the right path.

In 2018, I went for Albert Ocran's Spring Board roadshow programme at the Calvary charismatic Centre (C.C.C.) in Kumasi. That year, I made it to two of the Road Show programmes including the global convocation at the National Theatre, Accra. The seminar was inspiring and practical. I learnt a lot. I discovered a great and new window into the idea of daily, weekly and monthly planning through Mrs Pala Asiedu-Ofori (Corporate Service Executive of MTN). She talked about diversity and the "achily heel" that taught us about how a little weakness can bring down your whole perfection of career. After a beautiful presentation, a participant asked about how she combines parenting, marriage and her job and still manage to soar in her career.

Her answer was quite simple but helpful. Her secret is planning. She explains that she never starts a week without planning. She further explained that she never goes to bed on Sundays without her family schedules, routine, work tasks and deadlines and roadmap to attain them. With this, her week is already planned out and there is a need to waste time on unnecessary things. She added that time is scarce and only those who manage it well can benefit in the long term. If you want to win, learn how to plan and use your time effectively.

Pala's habit of not leaving the house before planning her weekly routine has contributed immensely to her success in many areas of her life.

WHY YOU NEED TO PLAN

The person who fails to plan accepts everything that is thrown at him or her in life because you don't have a choice. When you plan, it gives you the power to choose what is best for you. Embarking on your tertiary journey without a plan is like going on shopping without a budget and shopping list. You will return home with two troubles, an empty wallet and so many things you may want but not needed. A plan differentiates your wants from your needs that seek equal attention from your scarce resources.

Planning can never be relegated out of our day-to-day endeavours if we seek a forethought goal at the end of an activity. Planning is an advantageous means to be organised and guarantees an ideal result. If the idea is right but the plan is poor, the result will deviate from what is anticipated. It is advisable to put our best into planning because it is the foundation upon which your professional life will be built and if it is weak, you won't stand the test of time. A bad business with a good plan can win investment, but it will be difficult for a good business idea with a poor plan to be even considered for a review for investment. How well do you know yourself, what is your study plan and when is it perfect for you to study? Your plan needs not to only consider the books but should make time for other critical needs crying for attention. It is important to consider your routine when planning. Leisure, your sleep and spiritual responsibilities are equally salient.

You are a student for a reason and not as a passerby and with such a mindset you are clear on your goals. How do you plan effectively toward its attainment, how many "As" do you intend making at the end of your first semester or how do you take charge of your responsibilities as a student, etc. are some of the questions that should be answered before putting together a sound plan? This is your game plan, and you need it.

Follow these simple steps and draw a good plan.

Inquire

The informed man wields clout. With his knowledge, he can always manipulate the uninformed. Ask about your programme of study from church members, a friend, an acquaintance or someone you can approach. It will help you organise your way around and inculcate other needs to fit well in your schedule. A short course or a sandwich programme needs to be assessed to know whether taking it will not affect your overall output. A dance lesson, series of relationship seminars or a tutorial every Friday should be considered and coherently undertaken. Similarly, inquire and gather the necessary information about your course, church and others that will be fighting for your time and design your plan to suit it.

Put your Plan in Writing

When you write ideas, it distinguishes it from the millions of thoughts that run through the mind every day. If you fail to put it down, you will fail to own and implement it. When you write your goals, it will be gradually absorbed by the subconscious mind to help you achieve it. Own your plans by putting your trademark on it and accepting it as a guide. To make this easier, I have added a four-year purpose definition guide to this chapter. It will help you define each area of your academic life while merging with social and spiritual activities as well.

Your Plan should futuristic

I do not know how you might define planning but as a planner, I will touch on two features of a good plan. A good plan is futuristic and continuous. It is futuristic because it seeks to achieve a goal later; it can be just after reading this book. As an ongoing process, explains planning as always in action, thus we can return to the initial stage or continue from where one left or initiate a different face to sustain or relate to what has already been started.

Revise to Reflect

Your plan is like a business plan that needs constant revision to reflect the changing academic landscape. While you advance on your tertiary journey, things will change. I remember there were discussions about the implementation of the block system while I was in school although it hasn't materialized yet. Things may change and you ought to act accordingly. You can revise to reflect changes; it shows maturity and affirms the continuous state of planning.

PLANNING ON CAMPUS

Planning will involve day, weekly and monthly and semester plans as a student. In your semester plans, you set your target gradings, shorts courses, spiritual growth, personal development goals, etc. as a general goals plan that will be broken into daily, weekly and monthly goals on campus. The semester plan can be drafted while on vacation to give you ample time to put in the necessary details.

Your plan should look like what is represented in this diagram;

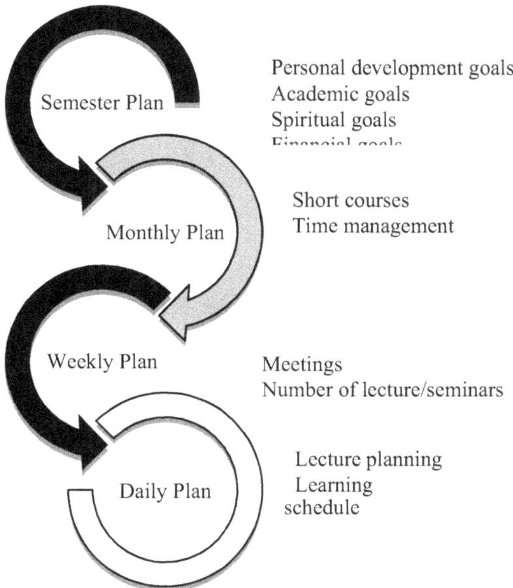

Your Semester Plan spells out areas of development including academic, spiritual, financial and personal development goals which will be further broken down into monthly goals. The Monthly Plan considers which of the semester goals is completed in what month. Your Weekly Plan should spell out the number of lectures, seminars and meetings as well as social activities you have within a week. This will help you apportion your daily time to suit each weekly goal.

Planning your day

Before you go to bed, list your priorities and activities for the next day, meditate on it before you sleep. To Savanur, your day is when you feel empowered and ready to make commitments towards your goals[6]. Your day is run by your energy levels and determines how far you will go. It is this way that you might feel enthusiast and willing to attend a morning lecture but reluctant to do the same with an afternoon or even evening lecture. Energy levels play key roles in our daily activities and contribute to how far we can make the mark.

To be productive and able to make greater contributing efforts to your goals, Savanur thinks you need to conquer your bed. You need to make provision for bedtime. Set routine sleeping time, develop the habit and follow it. It is good for your health and effectiveness. During such early mornings, your WILL POWER is at its peak. Most importantly, the will power approaches its peak when we do difficult things and depletes when we fail to do things which have been planned. At its peak, no task is difficult but perceived as a to-do that ought to be completed.

To me, conquering your bed is an important step toward being productive and effective. It gives you ample time to plan your day, run your activities with less or no pressure and most importantly have time for yourself, visualize and take

---

[6] Savanur, P. (2015). How to win your day. Vol 1.

action towards the attainment of your dreams. Conquering your bed comes with the need for self-assessment. You ought to know yourself/body. This in terms of food, bath, water, allergies etc. When you know and understand your body, you would know the type of meals that put you to sleep till morning, the diet that makes you heavier than you can manage and leaves you disorganised the next morning. I don't take more water in the evening because that will just increase my wake-up time to attend to nature's call thereby decreasing my peaceful short sleep-time. Conquering your bed too becomes routine and when you practice. It would become so natural that you wouldn't have to set an alarm to wake up at 4 am. You wouldn't have to relax to feel sleepy at 10 pm but because you've been able to conquer your bed. This is the basics of effective planning. You rule your bed for a bright, energetic and productive day.

During a freshmen seminar at church, presbyterian Church of Ghana, Salvation Congregation, Julia, a member of our youth ministry, asked an important question I would want to share the response the resource person gave. Earlier, the resource person had talked about multitasking and urged students not to engage in so many things. You will only become a Jack of all trade but a master of none. Also multitasking will just steal your glory. The key is, focus on one thing, get it done and move on to the next one.

Julia asked about time management and how she can apportion her time well to suit educational, social and spiritual and other needs. She asked that since multitasking is not recommended, how she can combine her education with a church leadership role. The answer was that, she can go ahead and take such a position but should manage her time effectively. Effective time management is important to get more done. Remember the 24 hours can never be altered to suit your needs. You should therefore, ensure that your week is planned and your daily activities are lined up ahead. Meetings should be on time and ensure that such time arrangements are obeyed.

Additionally, one could take advantage of delays to learn or revise notes similar to something I personally do while travelling. I personally keep shorthand notebooks (jotter) which I jot points whenever I am learning. Because it's small and easy to carry, I am able to take it almost everywhere and open it anything there is the need. Whenever I am in a car, I can just flip through and revise. Also, I can just open google on my phone to read more or research and jot points. So, you need to be also smart in your time managements. Don't visit google for the latest series/movies but also, research about your programme, course or new ways you can earn, or improve on your vocabulary etc.

Also, taking such roles and responsibilities adds up to the knowledge acquisition process while developing your leadership skills which is an important requirement on the job market

4-YEAR PURPOSE DEFINITION GUIDE (20..—20..)

Name: _______________________________________

Programme ____________________________________

Year of completion ____________________________

This guide will help you prepare your next four/three/two years to stay on campus to be purposeful. It is an excerpt of Pastor Mensah Otabil's 20-year development plan.

Defining Your Purpose

Defining your purpose makes planning more meaningful. The questions below will help you carve a dream, document it and motivate yourself to passionately pursue it:

1. What am I enthusiastic about or wanted to become?

   ____

   ____

   ____

   ____

2. What do I constantly imagine about life after school?

   ____

   ____

   ____

   ____

3. What will my programme equipped me to do in future?

   ____

   ____

   ____

   ____

Other Important Questions

1. How would I want my mates and friends to describe/remember me

   ____

   ____

   ____

   ____

2. What is my most important strength(s)?

   ____

   ____

   ____

   ____

3. What is my biggest weakness (es)?

   ____

   ____

   ____

4. What can I change about myself to make me a better person?

   ____

   ____

   ____

Personal Relationships Assessment

1. Which friendships have distracted me from my goals in education years ago?

   ____

   ____

   ____

2. What new relationships are needed in my life?

   ____

____

____

- *Remember: Friends are like elevators. They either take you up or bring you down.*

MY 4-YEAR TERTIARY GOALS

1. Educational Development:

____

____

____

2. Personal/Capacity Development:

____

____

____

3. Financial/Investment:

____

____

____

4. Overall Summary/Description: In 4 Years, I will be

____

____

____

My Personal Commitments for Year One- *Everything begins with a step upon which you will follow to achieve the long-term goals.*

A. Educational Goals *(e.g., I will complete this sem. with a first-class)*

1.____

2.____

3.____

A. Personal/Capacity Goals *(e.g., I'll develop my talent/ undertake two short courses)*

1. ____

2. ____

3. ____

C. Financial/Investment Goals *(e.g., I'll learn to cut unnecessary spending and open a long-term investment account)*

1. ____

2. ____

3. ____

Examples of Yearly Goals (For Various Aspects of Your Life)
- Read one book on spiritual/personal development every month
- Acquire knowledge in a field by self-educating
- Allocate 10-25% spending money into an investment

CHAPTER FOUR

HOW TO SUCCEED WITH YOUR PLAN

Succeeding with your Plan

In this chapter, you will learn how to go for your goals. With your goals, and a plan underway, the character traits you need to develop to help you meet each of them on the list is what you will discover in this chapter. They are the things you will do to armour yourself to take you through the tough moments to discover the true you. This can be a stepping stone to the apex of your aspirations not only on campus but in the future. To be able to realise your academic goals, adopt a success plan. From your coursework to spiritual life and social activities, you have to act to be on top of them.

Brian Tracy defines success as "...the ability to live your life the way you want to live it, doing what you most enjoy, surrounded by people whom you admire and respect"[7].

Scott Peck adds that success is not success in itself but rather it is a natural feeling that comes after the achievement of a milestone. When you set a goal to make GHC 200 in saving a semester, you would feel or become successful after being able to accomplish it. It is the same if you set out a target to move from, say, s (average) second class to first class. Success, therefore, is a feeling that accompanies the realization of goals and not a goal in itself.

---

[7] Tracy, B. (n.d). *The Power of habit.* Available at www.briantracy.com

To be successful as a student, you ought to set goals, draw out plans to attain them and that feeling will accompany when you attain each one on the list. Define your purpose, be determined and empowered to hold on to it, set goals and priorities, plan your timelines and that successful feeling will walk with you always because you will wake up every day accomplishing part of it. You will make good marks in your mid-semester exams, learn something new, meet and connect with people and mentors. In doing so, you will be gradually making efforts to attain your goals and also feel successful. Your plan consists of a series of activities that will lead your goals.

How to prepare and accomplish each intermediary task toward the achievement of each goal on the plan will be considered below.

Declare and plan

You have already learned how to define your purpose, challenge and plan it. It is important to your success as a student. To achieve something in life, you have to state and affirm it. There are many things you may envisage as the list of goals you seek to achieve over some time but you cannot attain all. This is why it is critical to declare what you need most and keen on its realisation. Take an inventory of your goals, select the significant ones that need to be achieved per semester, be devoted towards it and you will make progress. Goals are purposes discovered and nurtured. You declare and make it your prime target.

As discussed in the previous chapter, planning is momentous in life. You have to put what is required in place after you have defined your goal, to ensure it is achieved. With a plan, I know you have a goal as the result.

Set Achievable Targets

While you have set your goals and planned for the semester, you need to set attainable targets. What average do you want to graduate with? What course do you need to put in more effort? What areas do you personally have to develop? set achievable targets in these areas and work effortlessly towards them.

Work toward your Goal

Every goal comes with sacrifices and you need to ensure that you make the necessary commitment towards. You may need to alter your sleeping behaviour to make the class you have set for yourself. Yu may need to cut ties with some friends who don't challenge you to become the better you or quit a habit. This is what we call, getting out of your comfort zone. Your goals may not sync with your usual lifestyle but may require a new habit to be able to accomplish it.

Change the Old ways

Kerry Pendall said once that "life does not get better by chance but by change". Change according to Pedal attributed all life improvement to always take place inside. It is the alteration of your thought, the change of your old way of doing things, the ply of new roads or the undertaking of new initiatives that create the better life we aspire to live. You can't keep doing the same old things and expect a better result. There may be a status quo that you've become used to but you know that won't get you where you desperately need to. This is the time to make an assessment and start putting on the new leave. Even if you're the only one starting it, be courageous and keep doing. Don't listen to critics nor give up. Remember change does not come by day. Change is a process. Even, it takes at least 14-21 days to put on a new behaviour or habit of medium complexity such as getting up earlier at a specific hour, reading, etc. So, if you want to start reading more, you don't get there by completing 10 books in a day. Just do it every day, be consistent and keep reading till you wake up and what you want to do is read.

You cannot make an achievement overnight but consistent small commitment toward it daily. It becomes a habit and you persist through the bad and good days to make the change in the world. Although this may not happen in a day, you wake up every day with the hope that it will surely come to pass. You do this by making daily commitments, not in words but action to keep the spirit and hope.

In his e-book, Savanur elaborated how he manages to build software by breaking his work into helpful pieces[8]. He approaches every task with a feeling not to finish the bigger picture but how each smaller easy part can be built. Every day, you make a small commitment towards your bigger goal but taking small action on the breakdown of your purpose as a student. You need to relegate the old norm of waking up, eat, exercise, see the world, etc. and develop the traits that will make you feel successful. You cannot wish for other things while you continually go about the same old things and expect an improvement in your situation. Declaring what you need and taking the necessary actions to attain each one.

You need to change your sleeping pattern if you've been sleeping all night. You need to eat right and healthy, go heavier in the day and eat lighter in the evening. You can

---

[8] Savunur, P. (2015). How to win your day. Available online at: www.howtowinyourday.com

spend the whole night digesting a heavy meal; you'll only wake up already exhausted and hungry. You need to develop certain traits that can help you in your academic journey. Learn how to write, how to talk, be confident and develop the traits to suit your new environment.

Take Advantage of Opportunities

You need the bull's eye to detect opportunities. If you are not well informed about your goal, how do you identify a suitable moment from a distance? When you see it swinging in the air, take hold of it before someone. Open your eyes and ears and know when to make the moves that land the biggest catch. To win, you need to be passionate about a dream, know it, live it and grab it when the chance surfaces. By taking the challenge to be responsible for your new programme, you would be able to make hay while the sun shines. Our dreams are a reflection of our preferred future in wonderlands. An achiever makes the crucial ones while awake and able to communicate clearly to the mind a task to be achieved. Some people will go through a laid down medium to reach the top while others will meet challenges to get there. In all instances, we are just getting to our destination.

You can do it

You are blessed with the power to do exceedingly by directing your energies to accomplish goals. God in his way blessed us with this wonderful piece to help us achieve goals, therefore, you have to use it. Learn to communicate your goals to the subconscious mind and it will direct efforts to achieve each of them. One of America's greatest presidents, Thomas D. Roosevelt who happened to be a cripple always proclaimed that "the only limit to our achievements of tomorrow is our doubts of today". Your doubts can limit how far you can go with initiative. Your doubts are the only limitation to your achievements.

According to Munroe, one can release his/her true potential by restoring the original environment through their internal spiritual environment. Every goal is conceived inside and manifested in reality later. Learn to fill your mind with your success plan. Feed your mind with positive thoughts than to leave it ajar for negativity to be in charge. It is a process in itself, so you have to start early and be conversant with it. Meditate on your goals daily and watch it overtake your mind. This automatically gives you the power to achieve. The mind is always open to what it is fed.

Prospecting

Research your programme or the new skill you want to learn to Get in touch with those who can help you get. It makes things easier. Almost every challenge has been taken before, therefore there is someone who may have the experience and also, be willing to help you get there. This will be dependent on your networking skill which you will learn among the lessons. Your network should help you develop and elevate your status e.g., from an average student to an excellent one. They should be genuinely interested in helping you to develop. They should inspire you, challenge you to discover the best you or hidden beneficial traits. They will help you upgrade by teaching or helping you learn a skill, give you honest feedback on a presentation rehearsal he/she supervised. Their presence should add value to yourself and you should look out for those that qualify to be part of your network resource.

You have the power to choose who joins your network, so, choose well.

Be addicted to your dream

Is addiction bad? To me, it depends on what you get addicted to. In 2017, I watched only two movies. I had all the internet, unemployed then and had all the time but I was just addicted to other things that were important to me such as writing this book. What you get addicted to is very important to your success as a student. Your lectures, personal development seminars, reading, learn something new every semester, growing personally (physically and spiritually) and the causes that will help you become what you envisioned are what you ought to be addicted. If spending days watching movies is going to make you a career (such as writing reviews for websites), then that is fine, but just doing that for leisure is not advisable. Find your plan, develop the passion for it and be addicted to it.

Key 4

1. What did I learn?

____

____

____

2. My success plan?

____

____

____

3. How will this chapter help me attain goals?

____

____

____

CHAPTER FIVE

HOW TO UNDERTAKE RESEARCH

- *Getting started with research*
- *Research Approach*

A junior high student needs at least a mathematical set and a drawing board while a senior high student will need a scientific calculator. With your freedom, it is your responsibility to be equipped to put you in the capacity to accomplish your onus as a student. Assignment, quizzes, and examination require hands-on applications/software to get you through. You are in school to complete a programme and in doing so, you have to undertake assignments which give you the marks to obtain a degree/Higher National Diploma (HND) or a certificate. In this chapter, you will know what is required of you and how to search for information from the various sources to help you with your coursework.

First of all, you have to get a dedicated email address. The electronic mailing system is the primary medium used by lecturers to communicate with students. You will sometimes get access to lecture notes or handouts and even assignments via your mail. Due to evolution by smartphones and social media platforms, I believe you have one but in case you do not, you can create one with any of the providers; Google, Yahoo, Microsoft (Outlook, Hotmail, Live), AOL, etc. Go to any of the websites and register with a username and password. You should also do well and start checking your email handle frequently like your recent call list.

Your laptop or tablet will be an integral part of your day-to-day activities. It is no more for only movies and surfing the internet but for other roles as a student. It will now be used for learning, research, assignments and practical etc. There are packages on both Windows and Macs laptops which you will be using frequently as a student. I will elaborate on what you will need in the beginning to help you with your coursework. They are document processing, analysis tools and presentation aids. You will need Microsoft Word, Pages or Docs for your assignments and reports. PowerPoint, Keynote or Slides will be your presentations and tutorials aid while Excel, Numbers, and Sheets will be used in data analysis. You will be introduced to others like SPSS (Statistical Package for Social Sciences) while you move ahead. You can start now by looking for a 'how-to' book online, at your library on videos on YouTube.

RESEARCH

Undertaking a research activity is a complex process on its own which you will take as a course but it is necessary to get the basics to help with your coursework. There are two types; primary and secondary. Research is the systematic investigation into and study of materials and sources to establish facts and reach new conclusions.

> *Primary Research: practical, establishing knowledge through empirical approach.*
>
> *Secondary Research: theoretical, based on already published material that is, the facts of primary research.*

Let us consider a question and use it to elaborate more on research, the applications and coursework; the need for sports infrastructure in basic education, discuss. First of all, you have to undertake **research** and present your **findings** on a printed **document** using any of the above tools. Before a finding, there must be research to help you put together the necessary information and present it to your instructor. We will go through the keywords to help you understand it better. Resources one can rely on for academic research can be from different sources. We will consider credible and significant ones.

Websites

Unlike printed material in your institution or college library, these materials are online. Online resources include articles, web contents and various publications related to your programme. To assess these materials, one needs an internet connection to enable you to undertake queries on the World Wide Web (WWW).

Search Tools

Search tools are subject directories, meta-search engines, and search engines. They perform different but similar roles to help us find our way on the internet. Keywords are used for queries on the web using search tools. The question contains keywords such as sports, infrastructure, and basic education that can be used in the search. Just typing the keywords will return millions of results. One need to zero in on what exactly he/she is looking for when searching on the internet. This is done with the use of quotation marks ("") and addition sign (+). Entering just any of the keywords e.g. *infrastructure* any document or page listed on google that contains that word which may not be related to your search. Using quotations one can enter "sports infrastructure" +" basic education" to limit the search to documents that are related to the input keywords.

There is also a great tool called 'Google scholar' which is particularly designed to help researchers locate scholarly materials on the internet. This is similar to other search engines but its specialty is that it directs you to academic-related resources on different journals and research materials online. It is a great tool to help students locate such materials for research activities. To access the platform, log on to www.googlescholar.com and use the search space provided to undertake your research.

What to observe when using Online Resources or a website
When using online materials, you must assess and check against published materials to verify their credibility. The World Wide Web contains vast data which does not make everything there completely reliable for academic purposes. Researching online needs to be geared towards sources that are credible and academia related.

Steven E. Lucas gave out eight (8) checklists for evaluating internet documents. They are;
   i.   Is the author of the document identified?
   ii.   If the author is identified, is he or she an expert on the topic?
   iii.   If the author is not an expert, can his or her opinion be accepted as objective or unbiased?
   iv.   If the author is unidentified, can the sponsoring organization or body be recognized?
   v.   What type of organization is the sponsor?

vi.   What is the reputation (measured by objectivity and expertise) of the organization?

vii.   Does the document contain a copyright date, publication date, or date of last revision?

viii.   If the document has a date, is it recent enough to be used for my research?

These are fundamentals of making good research. You have credible and current evidence as references to back your findings/claims.

Information published on blogs, websites, and social media platforms are mere views and opinions which have not been scientifically proven. The popular online encyclopedia, Wikipedia, is an open-source library that can be used for research, but anyone from anywhere can alter it. When you are taking information from Wikipedia, I would advise you to go to the references section and refer to it. Whenever you undertake research online, try and verify from journals and books to ensure you are not presenting chaff to your instructor. You cannot use a post by your friend on Facebook to answer a question for your lecturer because it is online.

Books

The best source to investigate for academic purposes is from printed material including books, magazines, newspapers and journals, etc. which we can access from the library. Books and articles in journals, magazines and newspapers go through a series of processes (review, editing, proofreading, etc.) before publishing and are well classified under the codes used by the international community. They are mostly facts, no views and can be used to draw inferences from our findings when undertaking research.

Books and journals are located in the library. We will, therefore, discuss in detail in chapter 8 under the library as a resource. The material at the library will help you to undertake research and read further with course handouts. Lecture materials are a summary of lecturers' research. Therefore, you can delve more by visiting libraries for their sources.

Journals

They are materials published periodically on a particular subject or field. Academia related ones are good sources for research. A board edits papers submitted to journals and assesses it to meet standards that can be published. It is, therefore, credible and factual to be used. It is like books and more importantly by intellects. Therefore, it can be used for research. A journal related to a programme contains research by lead scholars to advance knowledge in that field. They are mostly field related but come together to form the general publication for a particular time.

They are available in print and electronic formats. Electronic journals contain a catalogue of articles and papers published by researchers, intellects, and students' researchers. It provides the platform to encourage and support research in a particular field. We have closed and open journals. Research papers submitted by researchers are published in a series of volumes at a particular time. Open access journals can be accessed on the internet by anyone e.g., UN–HABITAT, Journal of Science and Technology (JUST), Oguaa Journal of Social sciences, Elsevier, Emerald, Academia, etc. There are hundreds of journals out there, just look for those that are focused on your discipline. For access to closed journals publications, find out more from your institutions' librarian.

Also, student papers/thesis are published mostly in institutional repositories and are good sources for research. These could also be accessed in print at your library.

AN OUTLINE OF A RESEARCH REPORT

Any course work or assignment given requires some level of research. Thus, to gain insight into the subject and assist you to make inferences and present. A research report contains five main parts thus; introduction, literature review, methodology, presentation of findings and conclusions and recommendations. Although this directive is for standard research work, adopting it helps you organize your report to include all that is needed for the marks.

Introduction
This section just presents what the report is about, its content and how it is organised.

Literature review

This section is the revision of published work on the topic you are undertaking the research on. Read wide form credible websites, journals, student papers and books to gain wider insight about it then use the information to rewrite the chapter by presenting what you will find in your own words. This is where referencing becomes important and plagiarism issues emerge. Every paper or website or article you will take information from should be cited. You equally need to paraphrase your findings to reduce the issues of plagiarism.

Literature review equally is subdivided into sections. These are discussed briefly. The **theoretical framework;** this is the section where you will describe the theory (ies) backing your study. **Conceptual Review**; in this section, you will define the concepts, terms or subjects under scrutiny and link it to your study. **Empirical evidence**; in this section, you present scientific findings by other researchers. This section is important as this is what will be used to assist in writing discussing your findings. **Conceptual framework**; in this section you illustrate a graphical presentation or brief description of the relationship between key terms, concepts and other important areas exposed by the review.

Methodology

This section of a research report focuses on the approach used to conduct your research. Course work may fall under a review, case study design or probably a survey. This part describes areas such as the approaches adopted and population, data sources, analysis strategy

Findings and Discussions

Here, you have to present your findings and make inferences. If the study is a review, then this will be your empirical evidence linked to reality. Thus, you will present the findings of earlier published research and discuss. Discussion is typical to a debate on your findings to draw meaning out. What has been found by previous studies, are divergent views, any unique observation, how does this link to theory etc. are some of the questions to start.

Conclusion and Recommendation

Here, you will discuss the main findings of your study by linking it with your objectives and present to your reader any exception. A recommendation is a suggestion for the best course of action regarding the situation at hand. Its role is to propose a helpful direction that will resolve issues or shortfalls identified in your research as well as produce a positive effect.

REFERENCING IN RESEARCH

In doing your research, you have to keep track of all the books, articles, papers, sites, authors, and referred material that make up your findings. The use of other knowledge without giving credit is plagiarism that you need to avoid.

I believe you heard the brouhaha about President Akoffu Addo's speech he gave during his 2017 inauguration. His speech was cited to contain excerpts from George Bush's[9] speech which was originally uttered by Woodrow Wilson[10]. Plagiarism is like using Newton's laws of motion and making it look like you developed it all by yourself. It is, therefore,

---

[9] 43rd President of the United Stated of America.

[10] 28th President of the United Stated of America.

advisable to duly present the list of references for all research material used for your report. Reference is presented after your findings on a new page. Every assignment, report or presentation should be accompanied by a reference. Read more about Harvard and APA referencing styles and download templates to get started with referencing.

Key 5

1. What did I learn from this chapter?

____

____

____

____

2. What five things do I have to be remindful when
    embarking on research?

i. ____

____

____

ii. ____

____

____

iii. ____

____

____

iv. ____

____

____

v. ____

____

____

CHAPTER SIX

HOW TO PREPARE FOR EXAMINATION

• *Examination*

We discussed the examination in chapter two. This is your primary goal as a student. Examinations are a party to the requirements that will earn you a degree after the four or six years on campus. Whether a first-class or pass, it is dependent on how you understand, perceive and approach tertiary level examinations. The mentality and approach one will develop for end of semester examinations should be adopted for each. In this chapter, we will delve much into the grading systems and determinants of one's total output at the end of the semester to help you strategize ahead. Your plan should consider this and your success plan will help you achieve it.

THEY ALL STARTED WITH A DECISION

I sat in class with two alumni who obtained first class but on different grounds at KNUST. I decided to find out what was their secret to such a triumph and they did not deny our intrusion into their secrecies. The stories are inspiring and successful in themselves and I hope it will motivate and add up to what we have learnt so far. The strategy adopted by a student to suit his new environment is also added.

Priscilla, started the first semester with a second class upper and completed as the top student in her department.

She has been an inspirer and an adviser throughout the years we spent in school and continues to be there for me. Priscilla is from a family who motivated her, and the achievements of her elderly sisters kept her on the toes to take the challenge. I realised from her story that indeed almost every student is suffering or has suffered from the dilemma of the disappointing programme. Her award as the best student in the department was quite inspiring. I decided to probe further during this research to find out what transpired during the bad and the good days.

The key is a definition of one's self and the declaration to take a challenge which you will come out successful.
- Priscilla, KNUST

Priscilla narrates; *as a rejected Business Administration student coming to pursue a geography related programme, more or less with drawings was challenging. I decided to pursue it even though there was no interest.*

I said if there is a will, there is a way. I will just do my best. As my mum always says, "If it must be done, it must be done well". So, I gathered all my loins and decided to pursue no matter the challenge ahead. Sometimes I cry all day whenever I remember my mates were in the University of Cape Coast (UCC) pursuing business/accounting related programmes.

Every day after a hard day's lecture and workshop, I will weep. I informed my sister that I want to try Administration at the University of Education, Winneba (UEW), as it was a new programme they had instituted. I decided therefore to complete the first semester and leave but I do not know why It did not click again.

*I was disappointed with my results at the end of the first semester with D's I did not expect. With the faded feeling to give up, I decided to strategize by **studying the lecturers and know-how to answer their questions**. I was looking forward to a slightly higher average than what I had.*

I had to give up a role at church to enable me to focus on my studies. My mother told me there is time for everything, so I should study hard. She was my role model as well as my sisters.

*Things were not easy with the kind of friends I made. I decided not to study with ladies but guys because I chose to be at the senior high school, I attended due to the level of competition I needed. I decided to read and **do all my assignments the day I was given to ease the pressure**.*

I chose a hostel that was close to campus. It was close to my college so I could be there anytime there was a need and it aided my learning and interacting with others. **Priscilla Ankomah–Hackman, KNUST Alumnus**.

Another gentleman who was ready to take the challenge although disappointed with the programme did not forget the good student he has always been. He started with a first-class average in his first semester and completed as a first-class student as well. I admired his zeal and socialness. He never missed a gathering but that was not a distraction to his academic goals.

Daniel narrates;

*Accepting the admission was a decision I made although I was initially **disappointed with the programme**.*

It was better than staying in the house for a year and as I welcomed it, I needed to keep it. I could not go through a four-year journey just to waste because this will become part of me. A field I would have to represent in future when I graduate therefore the need to go through and be imparted.

I tried to be on top of issues but not let them weaken me. *I learned everything and try to understand what I could as well so that I could* **apply during examinations**.

The choice of study that helped me most was "learn and take everything seriously". I was not selective during learning; I considered all courses equal so I could triumph in all.

Once you are in school, make the best of every **opportunity**, *face everything with your resources by* **being prepared always**. *The conditions on campus will prepare you for the future so try and understand and face them like the end of semester examinations and you will come out successful and prepared.* Daniel Amenuvor, KNUST alumnus.

> *What you do with your free time is crucial and should be able to achieve the desired level of satisfaction. "The most critical thing is not to give in learning or academic time to others. Stick to your time",*
> **Daniel, KNUST**

Richard also narrated how he adjusted to the status quo in UCC and this has become a helpful means to learn and while preparing for examination:

Having identified that learning under pressure does not work for me, I have resolved to learn ahead of time. By this, I make sure I get access to lecture materials. I try to assemble past questions and lecture notes from senior students at the *department as soon as the semester reopens and keep records of dates for quizzes and end of semester exams. I had a **daily timetable** which forced me to always learn.*

*Quizzes that we write in UCC are in two forms, announced and unannounced quizzes. I made sure I read up to the last topic before the quizzes and solve all **past questions**. This is done at least a week to the date of the quiz.*

*Concerning exams, I always make sure that I go through the day's lesson before I sleep. I am therefore compelled to learn every day and as a result, by the time exam approaches my **confidence level** is high as I only revise my notes. I also make sure I go through past questions and have **group discussions** to upgrade my knowledge. Mostly, I learn from the mistakes I commit during the quizzes which help me prepare better for the exams.*

Richard Ahadzi UCC, Geography and Regional Planning 3

THESE STRATEGIES WILL HELP

Terms change from the state, give, define and explain to discuss, critique, justify which means more to add. A question does not just require a mere definition but what is in writing, what you think and how it is can be improved. In general, one should take note of the following;

Anticipate and Plan ahead of Time

Being time conscious will be an integral part of your way to the top. Be a student who sees danger and makes the necessary preparations ahead of time. Know your academic calendar, get your schedule underway and prepare always for a sit. Do not learn just for exams but learn to be able to apply after school.

There is no Final Examination

At the tertiary level, any paper you write is a final exam and what you get in an assignment goes a way to influence your overall output. The necessary preparation you will put in place before an end of semester exam should be adopted for others as well. Do not take rest in the early days of the semester to sacrifice at the end. The quizzes, mid-semester exams and assignments might be disdained, but they win the grades. It will be influential on what you will be awarded on your graduation day. A practical you have to prepare and bring along materials should be considered. You have all the resources and time to make the pass mark when given an assignment. You have one or two-week ultimatum, an open book and the availability of the internet to harness. During a quiz or mid-semester, you have just undertaken a few lectures which makes it easy to make the full marks. You just need a little push during the end of semester exam to pass.

Impress for the Marks

You have to impress to be rewarded. When an assignment is given out, everyone visits Google, etc., and reports are presented. In the end, it is the same idea presented in different wording. The marks are awarded to those who impress by adding practical examples, scientific evidence, graphics where possible, references, etc. You have to go the extra mile for the ultimate price. If no one impresses, the marking scheme will not be lowered.

If it is a field report, do not google for pictures, get genuine ones with your smartphone. Dig deep from journals, periodicals, think tanks, research organisation and books, etc. add credible references and justify your review. You might once a while copy or edit someone's work and submit, it is all part of school life but doesn't freeride on friends. When you have the time and opportunity, do your best and act like you are the only one meeting the marking scheme.

Do not overlook Past questions

Past questions are gold which is mined by scholars. Look for them everywhere and add to what you learn. I am not saying that is what you should depend on but try and get your hands on them since they might resurface during the end of semester exams and you cannot afford to miss it. I remember meeting questions in mid-semester exams and a carbon copy of them at the end of semester exams as well.

You can get one from the libraries and senior course mates. Read your handouts and research but solve the past questions too.

Be an Investigator

Open your mind to information in and out of campus. Ask questions about lecturers, what they demand from students and how they set their questions. When you are well informed, you run into the battlefield prepared with the hopes of winning but not just to fight. Mingle with the good students and tap into their knowledge. Assess how they learn and how it is effective for them.

Study in Group

Learning in groups and in different places helps improve the ability to recollect. One key in getting better results from your group is by forming with people who are better in what you want to improve. This will challenge you to become like them. If you want to improve on your academics, form such a group with some of the brilliant students in your class. If you need to improve in your Christian life, you do that with your strong Christian brothers but not your basketball mates. Learning with your group brings on board different solutions to the same problem which will help you during an examination. Form a study group with two or three mates and get it going. Get at least a lady on the team to ensure it is active and make effective use of time during meetings. Meet regularly prior to exams and discuss what you have learnt during the semester. Prepare well before a discussion and solve likely and past questions together. You can have time afterwards and touch on what you will miss.

Key 6

1. *What did I learn from this chapter and how will it help me?*

____

____

____

____

____

____

____

2. *What strategy do I have to adopt towards examination and coursework?*

____

____

____

____

____

____

____

____

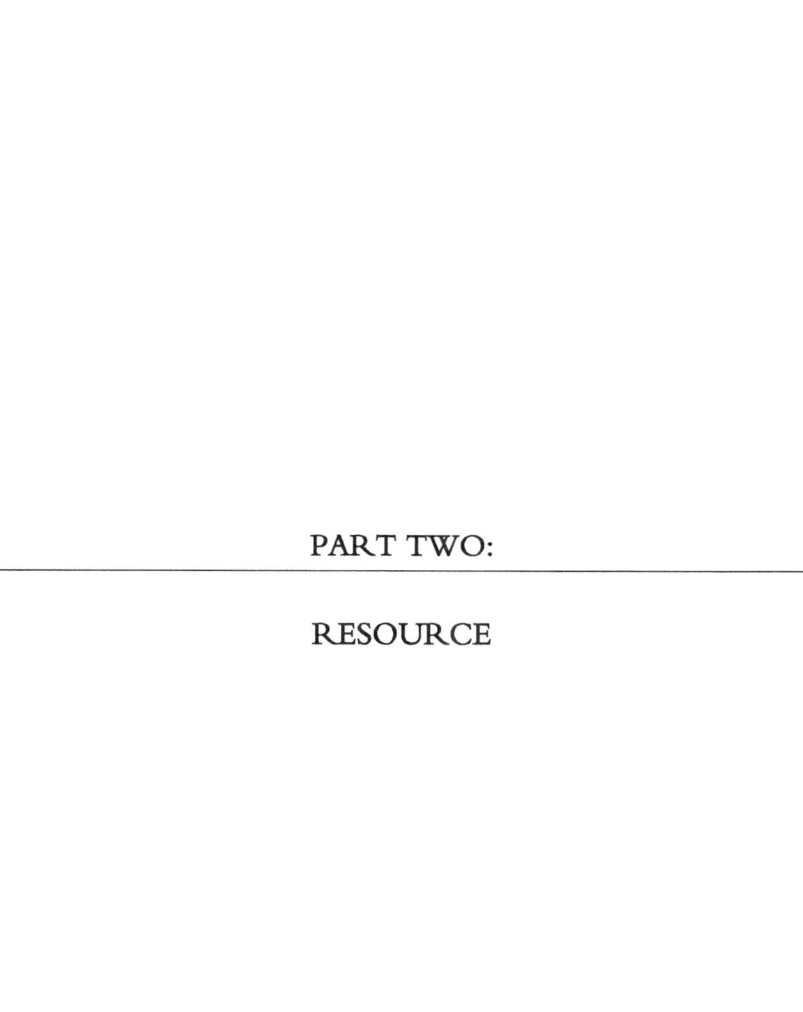

PART TWO:

RESOURCE

CHAPTER SEVEN

RESOURCES

* *Library*
* *Internet and ICT centres*
* *Scholarship and Aids*

Every institution in the educational cycles has a boost of resources to assist students. Tertiary institutions are not left out and outstandingly awash with these supplies. Libraries and ICT labs for research, conference rooms, lecture theatres, outdoor facilities and internet installations etc. are all found at this level. We will take a look at the key ones you would find on your campus and how you can benefit fully as a student. You need to be entertained, educated and informed during the four or five months stay on campus. I am concerned about the academic-related resources on your campus. Notwithstanding these, there are others for leisure, sports, health, personal development etc. which are pivotal to your stay and wellbeing on campus. Look for them and harness its usefulness because you might have paid for it.

LIBRARIES

The library is the most important facility on campuses when being a student is concerned. Students visit spasmodically anyway. A friend I met during the final year was at the library for the first time. It is not wrong considering the age of digital medium and technology. Now books are online, and everything can either be found on an e-book platform or the internet and in journals. Wikipedia, the free encyclopedia is open to anyone. The digital age is changing things and has affected published materials and books in general.

The library is a building or room containing a collection of books, periodicals, and sometimes films and recorded music for use or borrowing by the public or members of an institution for different purposes. Normally the main libraries are located close to residents on campuses for easy access while small ones are located at the various faculties/colleges. Libraries at the faculties contain published materials that are related to programmes pursued at that faculty. It includes special publications by lecturers that are directly related to your programme and can be borrowed for research activities. Your lecturer will be happy to see you reference his material as the source for an assignment. Libraries are put up to help students with research. Your school's library has its codes and regulations so do well and check on it. It includes borrowing and making use of certain special facilities on campus.

How to use the Library for Research

When you enter a library, the first thing is to check if there is a catalogue of the collections over the shelves. It assists you in locating what you need. The library is filled with publications on different subjects by different writers. Hence, it is advisable that you always use the catalogue in case there is one. Most libraries have a computerised catalogue to help you locate items. When you find what you need, walk to a shelf and pick the material and start with your research. You should remember to write the author's name, publisher, city and year of publishing and the title before starting the research. This will help you reference the information extracted from the book, journal or magazine when presenting your findings. Just go ahead and skim for what you need while taking notes. There are not only books in the library but also magazines, newspapers, and journals that we can use in our research, make sure you take note of the material you use.

How Libraries Operate

Most libraries open on weekdays and weekends as well. You would have to utilize your hall or hostel's study room in case you want to research during the off-hours or days. Some libraries have special facilities that enable students to enjoy certain services. Equipped ICT labs, research commons, and lounges that can be used for meetings and discussions. You might have to book or be a member of certain faculties/levels before you can use reserved facilities within the library.

The Balme Library operates a 24/7 reading room where you can learn till you do not "wanna" learn any more. You can resort to that if you happen to be a student at the premier university in Ghana. Libraries keep books to help you undertake research. Due to the systems run in tertiary institutions, you cannot buy pamphlets and textbooks (although you would occasionally buy for a course or a book that is related to your programme). As a result, provisions are made at libraries with the stock of books to enable you to read further on what your lecturer briefed in the class.

THE INTERNET AND ICT CENTRES

Internet provision is high on campuses due to its role in research activities. Students need the internet for research, learning and entertainment purposes. You need the internet to study, connect with friends and interact with instructors and course mates, etc. It is, therefore, necessary for the provision of dedicated internet services in the various tertiary institutions and faculties.

Your campus is equipped with internet access via WI-FI services that can be accessed for free or at an affordable fee. You might either need a little configuration or just a click to connect to enjoy the service. ICT centres are mostly located within libraries or close to them. There are other dedicated locations with WI-FI hotspots to help research and your hall as well. You can walk in and use the facility for allowed purposes. Special centres to help with your research might be located at your college or faculty so ask about it and use it.

SCHOLARSHIP AND AID

There are scholarship packages both international and local that you can take advantage as a student. It is provided by various organisations that you might be eligible to apply. Most of the international scholarships are geared toward certain fields and are not universally available. The General Electric Scholarship for freshmen is for students in the sciences and engineering field. Others like the MasterCard Foundation scholarship are universal and anyone can apply. Local scholarship schemes like the Test of Ghana Scholarship can be applied by freshmen and even if you have not been admitted to tertiary yet. Your department might have one for needy students. There are other avenues you can get help when you are in need. The various associations on campuses have designated support arrangements to assist students when they are in need. Your church, SRC, faculty or college as well as your Hall executives are available in times of distress. Some of the assistance is tagged for the needy so do not take the place of those who are really in need in case you are not. You might run out of money at times, and you can reach out to any of the avenues for help, but those that are tagged for the needy are for them.

Others are aids from certain institutions dedicated to ensuring your welfare as a student. The Students Financial Aid Office at the University of Ghana helps students by employing them to work on a part-time basis while on campus and assisting them to apply for scholarship packages from the various financiers. The Dean of Students' office is also there to help you, inquire about what you can get from there and benefit fully. Free counselling sessions and part-time work might be available to help you on campus.

CHAPTER EIGHT

ENTREPRENEURSHIP

- *Starting a Campus business*
- *What you can do as a student*

Undertaking a business initiative as a student may not be advisable but it is worth putting in the effort. A business on campus may not make you a fortune but will give you enough experience for life after school. I would advise on going into a partnership to flourish your business with two important things, the pool of (1) Ideas and (2) Resources. It will be beneficial to team up with equal minded students for mutual benefits. This will enable you to manage time effectively and equally fulfil your academic responsibilities.

It might be a passion, or a means to support your education. You can take a part-time job or implement a plan while studying and be successful with it. The university and polytechnic campuses are geographically populated during academic semesters which make them the largest residential markets you will find in the country. Campus market is like the forex; it never sleeps. There is a market for your campus business, therefore, do not neglect your passion or interest with the fear of losing capital. Get your plans underway, conduct a feasibility study to endorse your anticipated market and get it started. You can start small and grow to become a giant in the industry.

STARTING A CAMPUS BUSINESS

Thanks to the internet, you don't even need space to start a business. Just create an Instagram or Facebook account depending on your target market and start selling your products or offering your services. Every business requires capital so as the business you are planning to undertake. Are you partnering, being financed from savings or support from family? Try and define the means and do not stress yourself. You are limited by finance therefore try and undertake what is within your will.

Research about the Product and existing Market

What do you intend to sell to the student community? How do you get stock? Are you producing the product by yourself? If so, where do you get a reliable source of raw materials? What is the existing market and how do you intend to penetrate? What is the existing standard and what are you bringing new onboard? It will help you define and introduce your product and still be successful even if the market is dominated. Also, ensure that you define your target market. A target market is a particular group in which your product or service is intended to reach.

Starting a business on campus requires accurate market data to buttress the anticipated market. There is the need to go through a process to corroborate the plan of embarking on the journey. Production or procurement, sales strategy, target market, medium of delivery, personnel if any, and capital, etc. With concrete market data, you are set for a profitable journey and pool of experience. It is not always about the money but the need to take the initiative to open opportunities in the future. It can be an avenue to establish a network on campus.

It may cost a penny to conduct this study, but it is necessary for the success of your plans

Adopt a Marketing Strategy

The truth is that marketing is part of the planning process and resources ought to be allocated to its implementation. Make the necessary plan to market your offering to your target market. Networking is a key marketing tool. Make the necessary contact and sell your product or brand to the people around you. It can be for promotion or to try the new product. Your network will help market the product.

Students appreciate good customer services and freebies which you should take into consideration if you want to win a bigger share of the market. Branding also matters, so make sure you get your publicity game on. Services like door-to-door will put you ahead if the distance is a problem. Publicity will get your name out there, branding will present you differently, packaging will ensure your product is preferred to others, a good price will pull more people, excellent customer service will keep them coming back, and an add-on will convince a customer's friend.

Do the Business as a Student

Remember your primary role is to study, the business is just a secondary matter. The search for money should, therefore, not take the space of knowledge acquisition and you should never settle for that. Plan well by giving priority to your purpose. Do not skip lectures because your business is booming. You can get to your limit but not above. Do not be convinced by the money and remember you can hire an extra hand to help when the responsibility increases.

WHAT YOU CAN DO AS A STUDENT

Whatever, you can just be smart about it. Remember a business needs to bring in cash as more than it burns to sustain its activities. Smart businesses look for improved avenues to produce and deliver services/products. While finalising this book, I once ran into an old friend at work. While I was waiting for him to finish up my work, someone walked in and asked if he could take a passport picture. He gave him a seat and took his smartphone, snapped a passport size picture, exported into Photoshop, cropped it and transferred it into a portable Canon Selphy photo printer. He then charged him GHC 10 in just a few minutes. He is making the same money my uncle makes at his professional photo studio.

Printing and photocopying service

This is the largest market share on campuses, and you can even take advantage of not directly but on a mini scale. You can buy a Hewlett Packard (hp) 3-in-one printer and offer services to those on your floor. This one will cost between GHC 200 and 250 and can print, copy and scan or a GHC 120-150 one that only prints for the start. Buy an A4 sheet, which will cost around GHC 18 with 500 sheets in it. A GHC 120 printer and a GHC 18 sheet will reap you almost GHC 100 in income when printing GHC 0.20 per sheet. You can talk to your 'class rep' and take printing of handouts for the class and sell to the class at a commercial rate. You can also talk to your mates to print their assignment and deliver it to them in class. Just announce your service on your class' WhatsApp platform and you will be in business sooner than you think.

Vacation Travel

This is an occasional business and may not fetch you a monthly income but I can assure you that it will make you enough for saving or investment. Get a team together, plan, seek others guidance and make it work.

Food

Food is the business of no loss. We all eat and no one can forgo it. The task is to find what everyone eats and make the move. The increasing market for fruits and drinks can be harnessed. "Sobolo" has become the new soft drink, and we meet it everywhere, fruit cocktails and smoothies are also sellable. Socialisation, college and faculty weeks, SRC events, and Hall weeks are available for you to take advantage. You can take contracts from those in charge and make a profit on your service. If you are a good cook, you can make flyers and advertise it to your floor member. Prepare stew and soup on weekends and deliver to those interested.

Mini Importation

This is sometimes pursued as risky with the fear that goods ordered may not be shipped. However, several e-commerce platforms have emerged both locally and abroad which are trustworthy. You can buy just a screen protector for half a dollar, and it will be shipped to you. Sellers on online markets are reliable and would want to establish a long-term business link. I am not asking to be cautious but be selective in the websites you make business. Most of them do not have a buyer's protection plans, and that is the problem. Those who have that will ensure your product is safely delivered before releasing money to sellers.

This comprises buying online and selling to people. Mini importation involves buying goods in small quantities overseas which will be shipped to you. Items ranging from wearable to electronics, and work equipment can be purchased and shipped freely and sold for profit. There are thousands of products one can buy online. We will consider the processes, and you will decide on what to buy and the medium. You can buy in bulk and sell to wholesalers still at a profit because most of the items on these websites are cheap. Get either a prepaid card, a visa or mastercard from your banker. Other Visa cards by other banks in Ghana are accepted on these websites. Barclays Bank, Access Bank, UBA, and Cal bank. Just ask your bank about your card because Barclays has a different card for international transactions. When your card is ready, just log on to any the following websites, registers and start placing orders.

1. www.eliexpress.com
2. www.zoobashop.com
3. www.jumia.com.gh

Also, some of these e-commerce stores have applications and e.g., Jumia, Kikuu etc. that can be downloaded on your smartphone.

Work Online

By becoming a freelancer with the skill, you know already or what you will be learning soon.

You can publish your expertise online and help others achieve goals while you make money. Being a student gives you a handoff on emerging skills. Designing, tying, editing, PR, and so many you can capitalise on it to enough for savings.

Such jobs are online that you register and work either full time or part-time. Some of the jobs include data entries, virtual assistance, apps development online tutoring, graphic design, web design, etc. You can register on freelance sites and work from the comfort of your room. Log on to any of the sites below, register and start working online. You can check other ones as well, www.freelancer.com, www.fiverr.com, www.upwork.com, and other local freelance sites etc. What is important is having a skill therefore, I advise you learn through the knowledge acquisition chapter then sell your skills on these freelance platforms.

Blogging

Blogs are personal websites that you control and publish feeds to your audience. Bloggers publish material of their interest to like minds on their blog sites. You can also become a blogger by registering your account and start publishing materials related to your studies that can trend or drive traffic to your site. You have adequate and free internet that you can harness at no cost, why not give it a try. You just have to wake up early, surf the internet, be informed and know what is trending and update it on your blog. You can do well by updating with personal content regularly to educate readers and keep them coming back.

You have to act like a journalist and investigate issues before publishing to build a credible status as a blogger. It is easy, and you will enjoy it. Blogging will ignite an inquisitive spirit, continuous learning, research and the willingness to possess information. Bloggers earn money from blogging through traffic (visit). Local and foreign businesses can advertise on your site at a fee or through google advertising program (AdSense).

You could also join affiliate marketing programs and earn commissions on sales to your blog readers or organising training.

Forex Trading

Forex trading is buying and selling of currencies. You either buy by selling a currency in hand or sell a particular one to buy the other. You earn money in forex by pips, thus, the lot size earned on a transaction. The higher your bid, the higher your earning/loss and vice-versa. It is complex but a simple platform to interact and earn money in your free time by buying and selling currencies. To be the best, you have to learn and be awash with market information to help you make correct moves on the forex market. With your laptop or tablet and an internet connection, one can start trading on the different market at different times on the globe. It is a 24-hour market which you can enter anytime, anywhere and make money. The Tokyo, Sydney, London, Frankfurt and New York sessions will welcome you to be part of the biggest market in the world.

Caution to new Traders

Before you start trading in forex, log on to <u>babypips.com</u> (School of Pipsology) and undertake the lessons at the various stages to help you understand forex trading better. You will be taken through lessons as a starter and prepare you to be the pro trader you have always targeted. To become a profitable trader and benefit from your investment, you need to practice and be au fait with the platform before committing funds. You need to register and practice with a demo account from a forex broker (e.g., csmfx.com, fxpro.com) while you have enrolled at the "school of Pipsology". It gives you the feel of the live market and how to manage your account. The demo account is the same as a live account. Practising with a demo account will help you understand and prepare before opening your live account.

When you complete the lessons and finally assess your capabilities and attest that you are making profits on the demo account, this is time to take the necessary steps and become a forex trader. Just register a live account with your broker and start trading. Do not forget to use stop losses and a limit order to minimise loss. Internet connections, a nap at dawn can drain your lifetime investment when trading on the forex market. It is good to control the amount you earn as well the losses you incur starting as a new trader.

I will mail you a guide that has helped many in forex trading to help you through the journey. It will guide you to set up your live account and get started. Send a request to robertrexford@icloud.com with the subject 'forex' for your copy

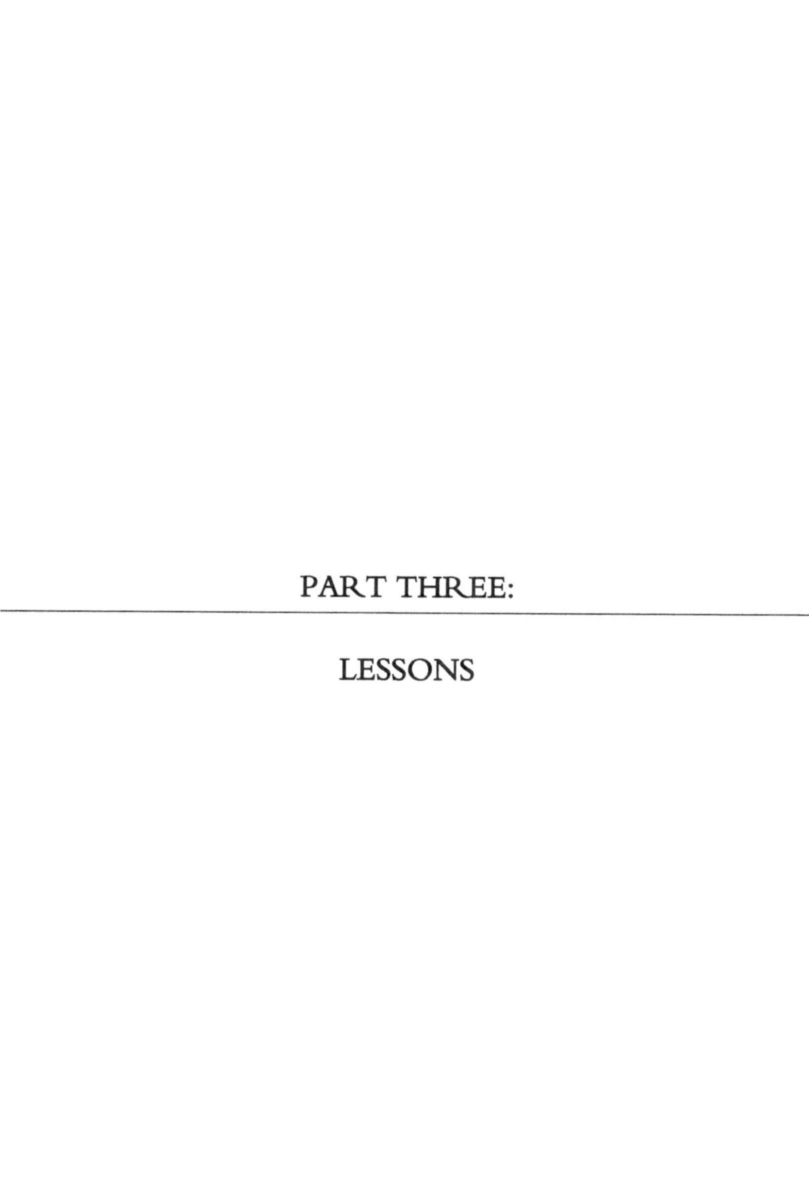

PART THREE:

LESSONS

CHAPTER NINE

ACQUIRE KNOWLEDGE

- *Talk to People*
- *Be an Agent of Change*
- *Learn Everything*

In my final year when I was undertaking my independent research study (thesis), I entered an office to administer a questionnaire. After my introduction, the man didn't address my plea but rather addressed what he saw in me. First of all, he made it clear that the worst he can do is not to respond to my questionnaire, and if I go out, there are hundreds of institutions/firms that I can administer it. His advice was that confidence is very important. You need to convince whoever you're before that you're not just holding a certificate but capable of what the certificate backs. As a student, it is not only the certificate that will take you far but other expertise that will sell you. You need to develop in other areas of your life.

You Are an Agent of Change

In our part of the world, the illiteracy rate is very high but we are still a unique group of people. You are different from someone because you can impart and effect change. You are trained to become an agent to spearhead the development and make initiatives to help the society adapt to technology and digital age. How will they benefit from the skill you will acquire? Or is it like how Mrs Letcher's parents told her as narrated in "Rich Dad Poor Dad", "study hard and get good

85

grades and you will find a high-paying job with great benefits" and that is all.

Our call is not just for personal enrichment but to intervene in the status quo and make life comfortable for the majority of the population. You will be the one to talk about the issues of concern but not to expect someone. The wrongs have to be corrected by you, and the initiation of change has to be championed by you as well. Will you complain when you see heaps of theses in the Head of Department's office? Yours will sit there afterwards unless you take your copy out and present it to the world like Fred Smith. He took his work to the limelight to create Federal Express (FedEx). FedEx is now one of the biggest courier services in the world. Yours is supposed to bring the change you have always wanted, but it can never be achieved sitting there. When Steve Jobs went to John Sculley to lure him to be part of Apple's team, he asked him a question to which he did not have an answer. "Do you want to spend the rest of your life selling sugared water or do you want a chance to change the world". So, ask yourself, do I want to change the world or continue to be comfortable with the status quo? You need to tell everyone that indeed, it does not belong there, but it was purposely meant to change the world.

The department will keep it there because it is the copy you gave them to attest that you did undertake that research. Anytime along the line, it can be just after graduation or a decade later but try and prove that the idea in your thesis is implementable. It will take time, but it is supposed to be strong too, a masterpiece deserves a master craft. You are the one who understood your questions, adopted a methodology and came out with findings so that the mantle will be on you as well.

AREAS YOU CAN ACQUIRE KNOWLEDGE

Learn the Art of Public Speaking

I studied BSc. Human Settlement Planning and my program involved a studio workshop once every week. Students were required to make compulsory presentations in groups or individually. Sometimes not the best students won the marks but the best talkers. You need to convince your panel that your point or argument is valid. It was one of the most difficult and challenging aspect of the program. Although, some students didn't see its importance then, it has impacted in different areas of our lives including conquering fears, developing confidence, report writing, effective verbal and graphics communication skills etc.

Job interviews are undertaken not only to test your capabilities or verify your qualifications but also to test your ability to communicate effectively. Why would a C.E.O put together high-profile expertise to sit and interview personnel? Why is it still important for an interview although you submitted a C. V. to your employer? Your inability to communicate your first-class expertise may not be able to land you a job. Nowadays, information technology has become an added advantage to job seekers due to the fast pace its development and prospects but communication skill has been the topmost personal skill required by employers[11]. The ability to stand on your toes and address a group of people is a great

---

[11] Lucas, E. S. (n.d). The Art of Public Speaking. 10th Ed. McGraw Hill, New York.

ability that will guarantee your success in most areas of your life. Most managers, CEOs, line managers and supervisors are regularly required to give speeches to their subordinates and followers.

Public speaking is often an imitation of someone. Find a speaker you admire and learn how they walk the talk. I am enthusiast about the content style of Pastor Albert Ocran but I like the delivery style of Barak Obama. Although I am still learning, they have helped me improve gradually over the years. I will share these avenues that can help you develop your public speaking skills on campus;

Join a Community on campus

There are growing vibrant communities/groups on campus where one could deliver frequent speeches to participants. Also, some groups undertake personal development training for members where resource personnel are invited to facilitate it. Associations also offer advantaged opportunities for students. The student parliament on most tertiary institutions offers such a platform. Honourable members learn basic communication skills to contribute effectively in decision making of the house.

Take leadership roles or join a group in your Church

I found this avenue as an easy way to get the opportunity to develop varied skills. Most of the leadership roles in churches are voluntary roles where you get the opportunity to undertake some leadership responsibilities including speaking. Here you can manage fear and nervousness when you stand Infront of people.

Other equal opportunities/platforms are available to you to help nurture your speaking skill while you're on campus.

Volunteer to presents for your group

Most programmes give students the opportunities to undertake assignments, term papers and research work which reports and findings are presented in class or inform of a panel. These are avenues one can use to develop their speaking skills on campus. You will be able to conquer fear and make convincing presentations when you participate.

Learn the Skill of Writing

Ability to write is equally important as your talking expertise. The same opportunities that talking can expose you, your ability to write can equally help. To be realistic, writing precedes speaking and talking. Your ability to write great pieces can make you a great speaker because you would be able to write insightful and quality content for your speeches. Some great speakers including presidents, CEOs etc. have aids whose job are just transcription of their idea into great speeches. Their job is to expand great ideas into insightful content on the subject matter. This is because they've learnt how to write. Everything that needs to become part of you, such as habits come naturally and through practice. It is first developed as a habit through continuous practice and gradually one becomes an expert in it. Research indicates that it would take someone at least 21 days to develop a new habit through continuous practice. You can therefore learn writing by adopting the skill and practicing. Use these as a guide.

You are free to write anything

You don't need a good idea or a great topic to write about. The first task is to develop the habit of writing. You need to cultivate the thirst to write something out of nothing. This can be achieved by trying something new every day. The habit can be cultivated through daily practice. What you need most is to remember that you have to write but not to write a great article or piece. Just remember, choose a topic or describe an activity, a place or thing and through this, you will gradually develop the habit.

My passion to write was unlocked while watching TV and a woman who happened to be a librarian or something like that *(sorry with my description but I just don't remember anything about her. I am still looking forward to meeting her)* said that you don't need to be a pro before you can write, you just need to remember to write and write whatever you want to write about. Choose your favourite medium, either pen and paper or computer and just start writing. The idea is to develop the habit, not to create great articles. You then transmute the habit when fully developed into creating contents such as articles, books, poems, website content, scriptwriting, music etc.

Specialize

Specialization is just a way to become a better version of what you want to pursue. It's like why you're pursuing program A or B. You specialize in writing after developing the habit. You then choose an area where you would explore and write about. It can be creative writing, motivational messages, etc. or anyhow you want to present your special talent to the world.

Take Short Courses

Microsoft Office, piano lessons and others that you can enrol for free or at an affordable fee or by self-educating can help you. These courses can help you in the job market while others will save you money on consultancy. Check your programme, interests and choose an add-on that will put you ahead of others on the job market. At least a course in I.T can help in various ways. You can take one in any of the programming languages (Java, Python, C++, Pearl, Script, HTML, etc.), online marketing or app development. An I.T skill gives you an advantage over others in the hunt for jobs. You can benefit by applying the skill to help improve or market your brand or for others at a fee.

The problem is giving a try, but that is also the basic requirement to get you interested. If you do not try, you will never understand, and if you do not understand, you will never like it, and if you do not like it, you will never be good with it. You will be required to use complex software/apps to help with your course which might be deterring just considering the interface. The truth is that each of these software/applications is like typing, your speed can never increase if you do not practise and your accuracy can never be better if you do not put in much time to practice. To be best is to consider its importance to your programme and what you will benefit from learning. You just have to download tutorials online and get someone who already knows to help you start the basics. You will become an expert. This should not end but set the pace to help you to learn more. You have to draw a timetable, e.g. two hours every Friday. Download pdfs and start teaching yourself to be that designer or programmer in just months. By mastering the basics, you will move up the ladder. There are free online courses on Youtube, Udemy, Edx, Havard and other platforms you can enrol and learn a skill.

Educate Yourself

"Through the power of self-education, you can be anything you want to be or do anything you want to do," Bob Webb.

Self-education is the medium through which you acquire knowledge by yourself without enrolling in a formal environment using tutorials or "how-to" resources. It is a form of self-investment. You can undertake a course online by following blogs or reading books on a topic you want to acquire knowledge. You have complete control over what, how and when to learn and which makes it flexible for you. Take an inventory of your capabilities and add a replenishing plan to work on where you need to overhaul. It can be every weekend; make the provisions and get the materials you would need to help you achieve that. An entrepreneur who sits on his monopoly will wake up numbers away from the first on the market. How do you see yourself in a year or two and how do you satisfy the requirement? When you invest in building your knowledge across other fields or upgrading in your existing field, you will always stay ahead of competitors

School of Dreams

I established a school in my personal life, and I call it the School of Dream. This was a personal classroom I would devote time to undertake a course I needed to enroll. It might be due to financial or time constraints that may prevent me from undertaking it in a formal environment. I would set timetables, prepare lesson notes and assess progress by asking others for help. This school has helped me learn so much that I could not have done waiting to be enrolled in the classroom. Basics of programming, web design, writing and graphic designing were taught using my classroom. I would get a friend already in the field to supervise or review my projects. Their comments, criticism, and suggestions will put you on the edge to greater heights.

Do not feel intimidated to hand out a piece of your writing, research or a video to a colleague to take a look. One might jibe the idea, but those who need to be part of your network will give you important comments to help you improve.

Hanes Cudjoe Sterling, IPMC Alumnus, 2015.

Lesson 1

What are the three things I have learnt?

....
....
....

What is required of me as a change agent?

....
....
....

Which areas do I have to acquire knowledge or improve?

....
....
....
....
....
....
....
....
....

CHAPTER TEN

NETWORKING IS A NECESSITY

- *Your Field Network*
- *The essence of Networking in School*

Networking was classified as a resource as key to the attainment of your tertiary goals. You need to develop it in school before entering the job market. Your network is your resource! With strong and reliable network resources, you can undertake any step in your career at any time. Before we go into detail of networking, I want to confess that this book wouldn't have been published if not for networking. From the idea conception to conducting interviews, research and getting people to review the document, all were executed through the power of networking. The last help I had before publishing this book when I was behind my set deadline was through networking. It was just a message to a WhatsApp group and help was knocking. Don't just underestimate the power of networking. In Ghana it is called "whom you know" but it is networking. It just works like that.

Before finishing this book, I met the fabulous woman, Ama Duncan[12], a network and resource development coach at the Fab Hub Ashanti and founder of the fabulous woman network. She had published her new book, 'networking 101' for students and entrepreneurs and

---

[12] Ama Duncan is a professional coach and CEO of the Fabulous Woman Network

I loved the book. It's a pocket-size that can be read in just a day but it is full of every detail you need to grow your network skills. How to network, the importance of the network, networking strategies to connect faster and more are covered in her networking "cutie" book. In networking 101, Ama gives an account of her journey as a housewife to becoming a corporate trainer through networking. Her networks have contributed to almost everything she's today and she doesn't joke with the opportunity to connect with someone at a meeting, an event or a gathering.

Gifty Anti[13] shares her network as one of the 52 bits that have accounted for her journey. The "whom you know exists". In this book, Ama calls them networks because they have spent time knowing the people they know. It is a form that benefits when they tap into when there is a need. Don't feel shy or demoralized to talk to a stranger at an event, who knows, she or might be your interviewer later.

A network is created to help us move ahead on a career ladder, open opportunities, develop personally etc. Your network should be the one that can take you where you cannot go yourself, reveal opportunities that you do not have access and help you undertake challenges that outweigh you. A good and reliable network increases your confidence level as you are bold to take steps even if you are not in the capacity because there is a resource to take you through. Everyone enters the institution as an individual but by graduation, some may leave as friends, associates, and even would-be couples and activists. Church, class, social groups, learning aids, are ways to create valuable networks. Do not lose it as most of us lost it.

---

[13] A renowned journalist in Ghana.

You will pay after school to get that network for one or two reasons. Remember enduring relations and friends are built at the tertiary level. Remember enduring relations are built at the tertiary level.

The first time I attended a church service on campus, I learnt that the members could ride in the church busses for free whenever they saw it on campus. All you needed to do was to give the driver a wave when you see the bus, and he will gladly give you a ride. I had been seeing these buses before I attended the service, yet, I did not know they offer such a free ride. Before you become part of a group, it will be difficult to figure out the subculture and what they enjoy as a group. Thus, being a member of a group in school does not only increase your network resource but also present opportunities to utilize whenever there is the need.

WHAT NETWORKS DO YOU NEED IN SCHOOL

Academic Prospects

Immediately, you settle, you have to start prospecting for academic networks, career possibilities and other important areas that can help you achieve your goals. You have to develop networks with students from other faculties, continuing students who are already studying your programme. Continuing students can be a valuable source of information about your programme or a course since they have already been there. They can share the ups and downs as well as the lecturers you should be looking out for and the ones you can take a break whenever you feel.

One other benefit to connect with continuing students is for past questions. Even if they don't have one, they can show you where to get it or tell you what is likely to make it on the examination sheet. As we already learnt in the examination chapter, past questions are very important to your academic success. Lecturers don't have the time to set new questions all the time and are fond of repeating them during the examination.

Professional Network

The convenient way to connect is through your class, department or college. This is easy because you may already be acquainted with some of your classmates. You can develop valuable networks within your field of study. Do not only make friends but develop formal relationships for career and professional benefits. Also, you can develop contact with resource persons you may meet through seminars, field visits, vacation training etc.

AMA DUNCAN'S STRATEGY FOR NETWORKING AT AN EVENT

In her book, networking 101 for students and entrepreneurs, she gives out tips on how to connect like a pro at an event. Her first advice is at least, go with someone you know already. With a partner you know already, you have something to talk about and be active. However, if you have no one to attend with, go early and make a friend or acquaintance before the event starts.

Get noticed by the speaker and audience. This means doing something active during the seminar/event or sitting on a front seat or somewhere visible. Being active can be note-taking, asking questions or answering open questions posed to the audience. As revealed in the guides section, note taking helps you understand whatever is being discussed and also ask intriguing questions. Asking questions gives you a hand to connect with the speaker or panel afterwards. This also gives you discussion points to connect when others after the event. People will want to say hello or thank you for being bold and asking their questions for them.

Take contacts. This extends the conversation and elevates the relationship developed at the event. You grow from acquaintance to network and so on.

Lesson 3

1. What is a network resource and how will I benefit as a student?

   ....
   ....
   ....

2. What network resource do I need as a/an .... (Profession) after school?

   ....
   ....
   ....
   ....
   ....
   ....

3. Describe your networking strategy?

   ....
   ....
   ....
   ....
   ....
   ....

CHAPTER ELEVEN

FINANCIAL LITERACY CLASS

- *Financial freedom process*

I have been an ardent listener of Springboard Radio Broadcast when it began airing on KFM in Kumasi every 11:15 am – 11:30 am and continued to attend the Springboard Road Show programmes. I have become a member of this wonderful life-transforming programme and I can attest to it; Springboard has helped me to get to where I am now. What I love about attending the programme is a constant reminder that you can save and invest wisely to become a millionaire in the foreseeable future. This analysis will give you what it takes and what you need to do to attain that and it is connected with age so you know where you are and how much you need to make to attain that target. I learnt from there that investment is not necessarily how much you put aside but how consistently you make such money work for you. It will take a twenty-year-old person to save and invest something small consistently every month to become a million but an adult needs a huge amount to meet that same goal because of the age factor and period of investment.

Graduates are unable to implement their business plans because of the lack of capital. The revolution is for graduates becoming job creators than seekers, and the way forward is financial literacy. Do not just draw plans to start a business but also consider its funding as well. It is possible and you can achieve it with decisiveness, sacrifice and dedication. Students need to be financially literate and prepare fully for the future. Save every penny you can, find a good investment house and keep it there, plan the business you dream of, find like-minded people and start the journey. You don't have to spend every penny you make but save for the rainy day. Whenever you are creating a hoax list for money, think about its capability of building a solid foundation and a brighter future.

I am writing this particular chapter to prompt you that you don't need to make the same mistakes we made. Knowledge, they always say, is power. Harness this power and be ushered into the great future you've always dreamt about. With this, I would like to present my lessons learnt regarding making financial progress from a series of seminars and training I have had that is working and helping me obtain a means to support my interests, initiatives.

RRAJ MODEL

I broke away from financial prison when I realised the need and importance of having overall control on one's finance. It was hard, but I needed to and with a declaration and determination I made a turn. The books I read helped me in accepting the need for change and learning to put on the new me. I learnt from friends as well to help me make financial changes. To be effective in making this decision you have to be true to yourself, be ready to take the financial literacy class, accept the need for change and start making plans toward it. The steps I took are as follows; I call it the **RRAJ Financial Model**.

FINANCIAL FREEDOM PROCESS 

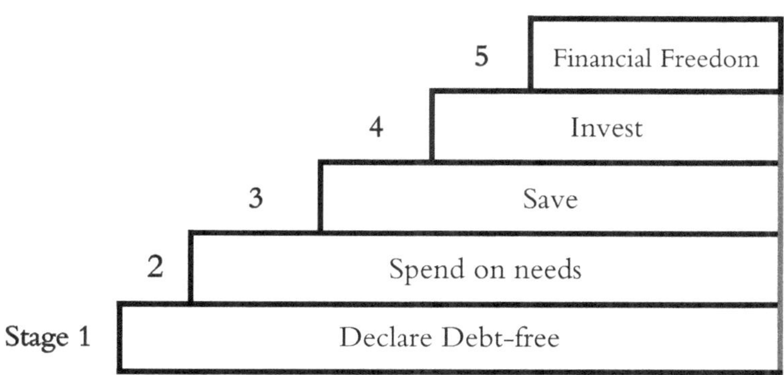

Declare Debt-free

With this, I settled my creditors every penny and retrieved every recoverable debt. It was the start of the financial literacy journey, and I felt free afterwards. Pay all that you owe and borrow less from people. If the need is not urgent, do not borrow. In school, you might run out of money sometimes and have to borrow from a friend to support you. We all survived on that but how long will you continue borrowing? As you gradually take the financial literacy class, make it a point to be free from debts. It is the basics of the course and accepting it will guarantee your progress. Borrowing will help you out of your problems today, but it will become part of you if you do not learn to cut it off. Assess your scale of preference, discern needs from wants, check your upkeep money and adjust your spending. You can never acquire all your needs nevertheless, wants. Understanding this will help you control your funds. You either have to control your spending or find a medium to raise money to finance your extra needs. The opportunities are there, and you can make your way out. Try a business by buying and selling items that your friends use or taking on a weekend job and the little you make can help the emancipation process. Just take a challenge towards financial freedom by managing your credit rate and finding alternatives to raising money other than borrowing. Do you want to join the queue of workers who always have to take overdraft monthly or the one who sometimes regularly saves a percentage of the earnings?

Spend on Needs

We have needs and wants in life. A want is the desire to acquire or do something while a need is a want that is essential and has to be satisfied. There can be a desire to own a vehicle, but the need for a vehicle to transport a load will have to be satisfied. Our needs are the things that are delicate for the undertaking of a particular activity, and its neglect can render the seizure of such activity, therefore, has to be satisfied.

Your wants today will grow to become needs tomorrow. In making financial decisions, there is the need to analyse the essence of using a particular amount in hand and the outcome. A desire to own a car today can become a need someday so as the latest iPhone you wish to get as a birthday gift. It will get to a time that work or interest will require you to have it, and you will need it. The best remedy is to cut excess expenditure on wants that fight for a share of your tiny income. Get a financial plan and monitor your spending either weekly or monthly or adopt a daily or weekly budget to help you save. A budget will help you allocate an amount to be spent in a stipulated time frame. It is a good tool for managing expenses and helps you stay within your income. Fads like phones and tablets and wearable will always put you on tenterhooks to spend. The iPhone will be updated annually so as Samsung products and other tech Giant on the market. The truth is that the latest will become outmoded so do not worry about your old one because of the new one. They will persuade you with improved specks to make what was great a moment looks worse with a good marketing platform. If your Samsung Note still has the S pen, there is no need for the latest release.

Make Saving A Habit

A key in the financial freedom process is understanding the reality and essence of saving. When you save, you create dependable insurance to draw from during emergencies. Your saving is a springboard to that greater achievement. Although your savings cannot make you a fortune in the shortest term, it will play a key role in your financial freedom in future. It is a decision which solely relies on you and a choice with no alternative.

No one would have excess income to invest in your dream if they had not set aside part of their earnings as untouchable. We all have needs and wants which could make way onto the shopping list as well. I read a testimony of Kofi Amoabeng, CEO of UT group before their financial crises. He needed GHC 20, 000 cedis as a startup capital but ended up not getting it, therefore he developed a strategy. He started taking small loans from many people to get that ransom needed to finance his business initiative which became one of the big locally-owned financial institutions in Ghana. There might be an idea no other person will understand (not even your parents) even though it has the potential of changing the world. This is when you would need those little savings to make the change. If you don't have the power at that very moment, your dreams can be shattered with the frustration of being turned down many at times and you might think no one is genuinely there for you but the truth is that each of them is practising that ideology you refused to defer. They don't believe in small growing to be bigger as well and choose to patronise their wants, luxury and others with their income although they are passionate and wish they could help. It is good and easy to spend what you have, but it is best if you can earn interest or a dividend to spend and still retain your ransom. I read most of the good books on the topic but to be able to develop that habit was to tell myself "it is time to save before I spend." Take a percentage out of any money you receive before realising your disposable amount; from there you can save.

I normally save for two reasons; either toward the execution of a goal or as insurance in the form of investment. When you always go for the former, you will habitually revert to the initial stage to begin the cycle. When your savings is invested profitably, it accumulates interest. The two are all in the right direction, but I prefer the latter because it can grow to finance your savings and you would need not to initiate saving toward a cause. It always serves as insurance.

When you save, it reduces the pressure on your earning in the future by giving you an alternative source for spending.

Buy a long-term Investment you can depend on someday

If you ask a carpenter on how to invest your money, I am auspicious he may talk about wood. A market woman may tell you something else as well as a mason. It is, therefore, important to consider how you seek investment advice. I will tell you what the banker or an insurance guru will tell you and then add an interesting investment option I have discovered and become addicted.

Investing on the Financial Market

It can be a pension from your first job, educational insurance while a student or shares in a company on the stock market or a bond that will yield interest. Investments help absorb unforeseen happenings in the future. It can be used to undertake business opportunities that surface while we embark on the journey of life. Invest your savings for a formidable financial future. I invested in a product at a bank and graduating from tertiary I had something to start my research when I developed an interest in writing. I undertook several business initiatives because I had the means. I attended seminars, training, workshops and breakfast meetings to increase my network resource whenever there was a need because I invested earlier that I depend on today.

"Investing to spend" will always reinstate you to saving but to be able to benefit fully from savings, you need to invest. When your saving is put in an investment for half a year, it yields interest, which might not be remarkable but for a longer period, it will cumulatively reap better returns. Through this, you will create an extra source of income and still have your savings to keep. Investing can help you plan your future or even leverage for support to pursue your master's degree after your first degree. Most long-term investments (like shares) do not yield much in the early stages but can rise as high as 60 per cent after the crawling stage. Talk to your banker and inquire about other products you can sign on and enjoy promising returns. Beware of the financial institutions that promise outrageous returns within a short time.

Investing in Oneself

The other form of investment I want to talk about is investing in one's self. This form of investment is making financial commitments that would have rather been deposited at the bank to acquire knowledge through training, seminars and personal training. There may be no tangible benefits in the short–term but in the long term. I discovered a greater reward in investing in varied facets of my life and I have not regretted. Its benefits are enormous. It is good to invest on the financial market such as stock, shares, treasuries, etc. but I recommend you put some of your investment not only upgrading to the latest phone or fashion but learn a trade, a course or how to deal with people and you will be glad you did. I attended a seminar back in 2016 which cost me just GHC 100. Later after my national service[14] when I wanted to finish this book, what I learnt was making me enough to finance my upkeep, research and investment. I still earn from what I learnt then. When I say invest in one's self, I mean devoting resources in the form of money and time to learn a trade, a course or handicraft that can expand your ability to make extra income. If you have reliable investment, it enables you to gain greater bargaining clout in business. You do not give out because there is a price but because an offer is worth the service you are selling.[15]

---

[14] A one-year compulsory service to the state for tertiary students in Ghana.

[15] Napoleon Hill, *Think and Grow Rich*.

Lesson 4

1. *What have I learnt?*

____

____

____

____

2. *What investment plan should I adopt to achieve the financial freedom status and further implement my business plan after school?*

____

____

____

____

____

____

____

____

____

____

____

CHAPTER TWELVE

THE FEMALE OUGHT TO BE EMPOWERED

Empower a female

The advocate for women empowerment has been in the limelight in past decades and more lately. This is a huge responsibility on each of us. We need to help the world achieve a common ground where the same opportunities available for a man are equally accessible by a woman. This quest is not a competition but increasing our expertise, abilities and capabilities to solve the world's toughest problems.

Becoming empowered

When Mrs Obama wrote about her life in becoming[16], she stressed on the need to cultivate values and believes in the upbringing of children. It is important to get the child on the right path. The woman, therefore ought to be raised by creating the awareness of why she has to take the initiative, break barriers and most importantly use her voice. Growing up, all she wanted was a dog, a house with stairs for his family and a four-door station wagon. Career-wise, she dreamt of attending to kids, a pediatrician because she just wanted to please the elderly in her neighbourhood. Despite her peanut aspiration, she has occupied one of the highest roles in the world, the first lady of the United States; a job she perceives as not a job because there were no official roles assigned.

---

[16] Obama, M. Becoming (2018). Crown Publishing Group.

Before this, she became a lawyer, a vice president at a hospital and the manager of an NGO that helps young people develop careers and many others. The key values that guided her through her journey which have never changed are what her father and mother taught her. Mrs Obama's father, Fraser, taught her to work hard, laugh often, and keep her word. Her mother, Marian, also, showed her how to think for herself and to use her voice to speak against the things she felt wasn't right. She learnt how to use her voice and keep a counsel of strong women who were inspired and dedicated to empowering her.

A bit of empowerment

In a 'bit of me[17]', Oheneyere Gifty Anti, as affectionately called, shared 52 things that have kept her throughout her journey and it's amazing. She has been through the thick and thin of life, been vilified, ridiculed and gossiped about. She still wears beads because she understood her condition and what she needed to keep her dream going, and gradually it became part of her and she loved it. People admire and love her just because of how she carried and improved gradually on that value.

The bits that empower and define her as a strong woman are her financial management skills, her power over her womanhood and the true definition of feminism, taking responsibility for her life and being confident and independent even after marriage. To her a woman who has been empowered breaks boundaries and accepts that she is capable of everything. She equally wields the clout as a man. You ought to take your future into your own hands, dream, feel limitless

---

[17] Oheneyere Gifty Anti. A bit of me. Amazon

and be bound to attain them because it's possible. To achieve this, you need to be responsible. Be responsible for every area of your life and most importantly make an impact in the life of others. One habit that has been an integral part of her journey is saving. She confessed that she nearly lost everything she has acquired in a twinkle of an eye except her savings. It became the turning point to rebuild herself after the storm. As a woman, this is one key foundation if you desire to be independent. The financial independence of the woman is a critical aspect of your empowerment. It sustains your faith and the power to stand for yourself and others.

I didn't know much about feminism before reading A Bit of Me, but she made it simple and reasonable. Feminism is just knowing your true value as a woman and human; "…what you stand for, knowing when to negotiate, when to compromise, and making decisions for yourself". If you need to be a housewife to your future husband, it should be your own decision to do that but not a coercion or society's stereotype that will put you there. In all this, you ought to "own your v, young lady". It is very important how you will narrate your first encounter with a man. Will it be with your husband, a hook-up, or just a one-night stand? Even if we take religion and beliefs aside, will you be proud of that man you will give that precious part of you to after ten or twenty years down the line. Don't feel intimidated, pressured to give it in neither should it be seen as your most valuable item that can get you the best in life.

You have the potential to go for what you want although the road might be tough, you can make it. There is more testimony like her, Gifty Anti, to give you hope for the future.

When you talk about achievements at the tertiary level, women have also made an outstanding contribution and remarkable accomplishment. In 2016, Dr Fathia Karim became the first-ever most awarded student at the Komfo Anokye Teaching Hospital. She won 12 out of the total 15 awards on offer including the Hoffman Specks Honorary that has never been won by a woman since its inception in 1996. Her achievement was seen as remarkable considering the domination of men in that sphere. A similar incident happened when a former Yaa Asantewaa Girls SHS student, Dr Ellen Boakye won 10 awards from the University of Ghana Medical School. Would they have achieved these; If they were afraid, unempowered, limited or did not know their power and worth nor understand their capabilities. Would the world have ever witnessed such a milestone? It may only take a woman to bring forth such accomplishment[18] and limiting women means holding the world back for a moment.

If you are a lady, know that you can achieve whatever you have set for yourself. If you are a male, empower a female not because you are interested in her but because you will make the world a better place. The world needs more experts to solve our problems. Be that motivator today!

---

[18] Nana Konadu Agyeman Rawlings, *it takes a woman*. Woeli, Accra.

PART FOUR

GUIDES

ASSIGNMENTS/COURSEWORK GUIDE

You may be given a week or two to submit an assignment. The internet and the libraries are available; therefore, this is where you can make the marks. When you make between 25 and 30%, all you need is a 45 or 55% for an A or 20% to pass during the end of semester examination. Most often, students wait till end of semester exams that they need to read all the accumulated handouts to make the marks. However, during exams, you will not have access to study materials but face strict supervision and in that case, you will only write to barely pass.

You may procrastinate when given an assignment only to realise it's almost deadline therefore, look for just anything you lay your hands on online or dab form a colleague and submit. However, if you put much effort into it, you can present credible information to your lecturer and get the maximum marks which will get you closer to your academic goal.

Use the format given under 'how to undertake research' in chapter five as a guide. Also, take the following into consideration whenever you have a pending assignment to be able to meet a deadline with good content;

1. Do a quick research online just after the lecture or after your siesta. Visit Google or Yahoo and ascertain the general knowledge in the topic and save the pages for further reference.

2. Go to the library if necessary, for any referrals on the internet or from your lecturer's handout. Get trusted and

facts from books or journal articles to support your argument or points that will be raised in the report. Remember to write your references.

3. Rewrite the structure of your report. After gathering the information, put points down which will be used for the report. After this just give yourself time and think through your findings, the points being presented and how you will conclude. This helps you present a unique view on the subject everyone will be working on and from almost the same source.

4. Conclude your report and you are good to submit in time with the report that will win the marks. Also, reduce verbatim copying and increase the use of your own words.

PRESENTATION GUIDE

Presentation skill is key to your success as a student and will prepare you to become a good communicator after school. You may represent your company at corporate meetings and taking a lesson now will be worth it then. The two elements to consider when preparing for a presentation is the content and delivery. Your presentation deserves to communicate, connect and effectively deliver a message. You need to put in much effort to achieve that. If it is an integral part of your programme, then learn it well. The first rule to consider when preparing for your presentations is to understand that the panel (and audience) is there to support you. They want to make your work/idea better. They are not there to condemn you but to constructively criticise to help improve your work. You need the comments of the experienced lecturers to help you improve. Whenever you have one, do not panic but just prepare well. No one can start as a master, but practising will make you one. Therefore, appreciate your mistakes in the start and work on it. Take note of the following to improve your presentation skills. Note this is also a form of public speaking, therefore, combining this with the section in chapter nine (9) will help you improve on your presentation skills.

Write a Guide

To overcome fear and not be intimidated, craft how you expect the presentation to go. With a guide, you can connect with the panel by following a pattern or developing the story from beginning to the end.

Rehearse

With a guide and a well-crafted message, it will be perfect to give it a try before the official presentation. Rehearsing will help you improve on delivery and communicate effectively. You will be able to select appropriate words and terminologies best for the topic to convince your panel. It can help you overcome fear and increase your confidence level.

Present Credible Information

The content of your slides is vital to the success of the presentation. It will determine if you will excel, fail or face difficult questions. Your lecturers are intellectuals, and you cannot deceive them with chaff. They have an idea of what you will be presenting therefore be genuine with your content.

Talk about what you know and convince them with the little you know so they can help you with the more you do not know. Remember they are there to help.

Be Confident and Run Your Show

You need to use your natural conversational tone to be able to deliver effectively. This will boost your confidence level. You have to be bold to convince your panel. Do not be shaky or go easily to retract what you know (not what you think) is right. You stand to be a leader or a public officer in future; therefore, the training is to make you a great one. Convince your panel with your courage, charisma, persona and energy.

Relax and Do Your Best to Be the Best

The audience, examiners are there to help you make a better presentation. *Do not panic to see a panel or crowd but be happy to see a hall of supporters who want to see you succeed.* Your audience have made time just to watch you speak while your panel want to help you improve, therefore, do not be adversely affected by the presence of your mates or tutors. Anytime you are caught in the hot seat, take a deep breath and tell yourself; I can do this.

GROUP ETHICS/TEAMWORK

One common tradition at the tertiary level is working with others. Working together among students in the form of groups helps achieve a common goal that benefits one another. Human beings were created as social animals and therefore I expected to work hand in hand with others for the common good of the group. God even created the universe by expressing creation by the means of a combined work of the Father, Son and the Holy Spirit. In Genesis 1:26, reads "Then God said, "Let us make man in our image, in our likeness". The "us" gives us evidence that there was a team at work. Teamwork is ideal for the fulfilment of purposes as students.

Groups/teams do not only create the need to interact with others but the utmost benefit for students. Developing a good relationship with your group members helps you develop personally thus understand how to work with people, improve knowledge, appreciate and learn from others. You might initially run into arguments and even brawls with a member(s) in the initial stages but it is the basics of every healthy relationship. It helps you appreciate your differences and build a stronger bond through the appreciation of group dynamics. In the Theory of Leadership, Myles Munroe gave some codes for healthy groups. These are modified below;

Codes for Successful/Healthy group Relationships:
- The leader of the group should be respected and supported for a healthy relationship and benefits.
- Build external networks to help with problems that supersede the groups' ability.
- Prepare meetings/work plans.
- Tolerate/respect others' view to create a comfortable, related atmosphere.
- Solve problems effectively and amicably.
- Define each member's role.
- Communicate and decide by agreement.
- Access team progress and honour achievements.

Stephen Lucas also in the tenth edition of the Art of leadership went further to add individual codes for small groups.

Responsibilities in groups

- Commit yourself to the objectives of the group or task at hand.
- Be a team player
- Do individual assignment or task given
- Avoid interpersonal conflict
- Encourage full participation
- Keep meeting on the topic/agenda of the day by avoiding distractive conversations.

Members should collectively ensure that codes are upheld. Group members should, therefore, adhere to these personal codes for the effective delivery of goals. The success of groups helps in the personal development of individual members. Members of healthy groups are disciplined and find it easy relating to people to create networks. Academically, they can also improve because the good students in the group can lift the average one. If the group scores higher marks, all members benefit collectively, no matter their intelligence levels or abilities. Members can ask questions, share individual experiences and expertise to help in their personal development of members as well. Being a good team player can enhance your C.V. and play a key role in your success in the corporate world.

KNOW YOUR LECTURER

Some lecturers will demand more from you along with results while others will leave you to be on your own but will expect results. Others will always be on your neck but will hardly give you a fail.

Every lecturer has a way of setting his/her question and how he wants you to answer them. Is he the "research and give me more" type, the "produce what I gave you" type or the "apply what I taught you" one? Each of them needs to be understood. When you have to apply what you learnt about a topic in a real-life situation, it is like an interview, you might struggle before you can navigate to the answer he or she is expecting. The research type will not give you much in the class, but the salient and intriguing points for you to read more. Their assignments are always asking you for more or help establish knowledge on a particular topic with your research. The one that will ask you to produce what they taught you will be on your neck. You read and understand but you cannot bring onboard something anew from a book you read. If the question is *what is motion?* You have to answer with Newton's definition or you are doomed. You are confined to delve for information to help you understand more. You might meet just a few of these.

When you meet a lecturer for the first time, do not just admire him or her. Access the lecturer based on his or her capabilities, how he orders the class, his choice of words, how he relates examples to course content and reacts to misconducts in the class. Taking note of these will give you a clear picture of how to act under his watch. Some lecturers will not even smile and lateness can never be entertained therefore make sure you are there before anyone or don't show up for the humiliation. When the attendance is taken daily then there is trouble in the air, you skip three times continuously and you need to pen a formal letter.

An Experience

I once had a lecturer whom I carry his memories all the time. Before he would take his first class, two lecturers came to have a talk with my class. We were urged to do our best as students. I inquired about the history and found that things did not augur well between a previous class and him. He denounced his interest to teach subsequent students of my programme and we were the first class he would teach after reinstating his interest, therefore, the need for such alert and honourable introduction.

He finally reported and as usual, lectures started on a good and very healthy note. He was punctual, straight forward and commanded the class with ease. His practical sections were almost a whole day on the field and as cautioned students, we submitted without question. However, he did not entertain lateness and misconduct in class. Whoever failed to comply is dealt with accordingly. Through these encounters, I realised he was someone who treated students equally, was disciplined, stood by his words and tried his best to help students acquire the knowledge he seeks to impart. Students feared and hated him for not being lenient at times. He would use his personal experiences to advise us sometimes, which made him a father figure to me.

He simply did not entertain mediocrity, laziness and average input from students taking his course. What I liked about him was that he keeps names. This is how I assessed an encounter with one professor that helped me understand him well and completed his course successfully.

Academic Supervisor

You would be given a father figure on campus to assist you academically. As a freshman or continuing student, you might encounter problems with a course, offend another lecturer or anything relating to academics which might be beyond you. This is where he comes in as your advisor. His role is to help you make the best decisions by guiding you with his experience and expertise. Students most at times do not make use of this opportunity and go around searching for help from colleagues and others who might not be in the position to help.

When your academic supervisor is assigned, go to him or her and find out how the relationship should be, discuss his role, get acquainted and develop a rapport. When this is established, you have to ask for his/her contact (mobile/office and email address) for intermittent exchanges. His contact number is for emergencies and the mail should be the main medium to get to him. I think it is the best because you would be more comfortable discussing important matters concerning academics with him/her through that medium.

LIFESTYLE AND RELATIONSHIPS ON CAMPUS

This is an important aspect or area in the tertiary students' lifestyle. I am no expert on relationships and I do not seek to give you relationship advice but just to share with you real life events to serve as a guide. Sometimes you just don't need expert advice but just observe the story unravel. I will share some stories to give you a gist of the relationship at this level.

The first love story I would share with you is about Kelvin and Matilda who become lovers a few weeks on campus. *They fell in love with each other and never missed* any of the beautiful outings on campus. They went to the parties, were there for each other and shared beautiful moments. But the lady was carried by the fantasies and forgot her purpose as a student. They were sharing beautiful moments but forgot to share study times. At the end of their first academic semester, Matilda trailed some papers while the Kelvin did not and when she found out she never talked to him again.

The second story is about Alfred, a fine fair gentleman, who dated three ladies in just one department. *He dated a mate in his first year, a junior mate later and another course mate of his first girlfriend intermittently. What is different about Alfred story is that he had a serious girlfriend off campus who was his everything however, he was mingling almost every semester.*

Alice's story is shot. *Alice had dated Kwame for four years but ended up marrying someone else just few months after graduating. Kwame still had plans for their relationship but Alice had otherwise.*

The last story is about two students who rivalled and later became lovers. This is how Kwame narrated his story; *I met Evelyn in class one day while we were working on an assignment for a presentation when I had to borrow a mathematical instrument from a mate forgetting it was mine. I was met with harsh words which raised tempers and I had to leave the studio and continue another time. I was distant for some time until her friend became my group member. We later became acquaintances and friends. We did our thesis together. In the later part of our final semester, she had a re-sit and I lent her my notes and spent time at the library with her. I didn't realise these gestures have touched her heart. We dated after school and got married later.*

What I know is that most of us come here already engaged in complex and pressure-induced relationships so don't rush with this. Concentrate on your purpose as a student and love will come knocking on your door at the right time. If you get into one don't be blinded by the gestures and don't give in anything you will regret after a breakup.

I would advise that you stick to whatever your belief is, thus if you're a Christian or Muslim, follow the teachings, it saves most time, troubles and unnecessary heartbreaks. Talk to your parents about your relationships but not only your friends. Sometimes it is hard to do this when you have not had such bond. They have the experience and care more about you than anyone so they are willing to give you the best advice.

Sometimes you need to take some time off the books and ease the stress. It is important for the body. Kwame may watch movie two hours every day while you take every other weekend off to ease the stress. What works for you is fine and don't be intimidated by someone seriousness if yours is working for you though, be challenged at times. Set free times to attend to other needs off the books. Make merry during such time but don't trade the book times.

AFTERWORD

In all things seek God first. Your success does not depend only on your books but God's will for you. I pray he opens your mind to understand the content of this book and apply accordingly. RRAJ's Guide for freshmen is just a book with a purpose; therefore, I entreat you to make it fruitful. There are different people from different homes on your campus, therefore, do not be drowned by the tertiary culture. You will graduate like how you graduated from High School and might not see a mate again.

Find a purpose that will drive your passion to attain success. There is no magic, others have made their mark through hard work, determination and persistence. You can emulate the examples presented in this book and your story will be next. May God bless you and make your plans fruitful.

REFERENCES

SCRIPTURE

p. 68: "And God said, let us make man in our image, after our likeness"- Genesis 1:26 (*NKJV*)

INTRODUCTION

Munroe, M. (2011). *Spirit of leadership.* Whitaker house New Kensington

Warren, R.   (2002). The Purpose Driven Life. Zondervan, Michigan

PART ONE

Tracy, B. (2007) *Time power.* AMAKOM/American Management Association NY

Dodge, J. S. (2016) Unpublished interview conducted by Robert Rexford Jnr, 20 July.

Murphy, J. (2001). *Power of the subconscious mind* Bantam; Revised edition

Hill, N. (2004) *Think and Grow Rich: The 21st-Century Edition* The High Roads media.

Amenuvor, D. (2016) Unpublished interview conducted by Robert Rexford Anim Jnr, 25 September 2016.

Ankomah-Hackman, P. (2016) Unpublished interview conducted by Robert Rexford Anim Jnr, 11 September 2016.

Richard, A. (2016) Unpublished interview conducted by Robert Rexford Anim Jnr, 20 July 2016.

{http://www.lifetimequotes.com} (06 July 2016)

{http://www.thesecret.tv} (September 2012, March 2015, September 2016)

Glenn Parker, *Teamwork* (Successories Library Inc., 1998), 4–40: chapter headings.

Munroe, M. (2011). *Spirit of leadership.* Whitaker house New Kensington

PART TWO

{http://knust lib http://library.knust.edu.gh/} (20 August 2016)

{http://mcf.knust.edu.gh/} (11 August 2016)

{http://www.ug.edu.gh/aid/the–GE-Scholarship} (20 August 2016)

{http://www.ug.edu.gh/aid/welcome} (21 August 2016)

{https://ghana.usembassy.gov/niv_application.html} (20 August 2016)

{https://www.gov.uk/apply-uk-visa} (20 August 2016)

{http://www.vfsglobal.com/SouthAfrica/Ghana/holiday.html} (21 August 2016)

{http://www.emirates.com/ae/english/plan_book/essential_information/visa_passport_information/prearranged_uae_visas.aspx} (20 August 2016)

{http://www.nairaland.com/1586538/5-profitable-businesses-student-venture} (24 September 2016)

{http://www.babypis.com} (15 February, 2016)

PART THREE

Steve Jobs. (2015). [DVD] Hollywood: Danny Boyle. Universal Pictures

Kiyosaki, R. and Lechter, S. (2000). Rich dad, poor dad. New York: Warner Business Books.

{http://www.silicon-valley-story.de/sv/apple_sculley.html} (24 September 2016

Larry, K (2008). How to talk to anyone, anytime, anywhere

{http://www.tutorialspoint.com} (20, 22 March 2016)

{https://yali.state.gov/courses/personal-growth-1/} (15 September 2016)

{https://yali.state.gov/courses/personal-growth-2/} (15 September 2016)

{https://yali.state.gov/courses/starting-biz/} (15 September 2016)

Hill, N. (1972). Think and grow rich action manual. New York: Hawthorn.

Kiyosaki, R. and Lechter, S. (2000). Rich dad, poor dad. New York: Warner Business Books.